REV TOBIAS HARTWELL

ST.AGNES OF ROME

A Journey Of Purity, Power, And Persecution.

Copyright © 2024 by Rev TOBIAS HARTWELL

All rights reserved. No part of this publication may be reproduced, stored or transmitted in any form or by any means, electronic, mechanical, photocopying, recording, scanning, or otherwise without written permission from the publisher. It is illegal to copy this book, post it to a website, or distribute it by any other means without permission.

Rev TOBIAS HARTWELL asserts the moral right to be identified as the author of this work.

First edition

This book was professionally typeset on Reedsy.
Find out more at reedsy.com

Contents

Introduction	1
A Journey Through Light and Shadow	1
THE EARLY YEARS: A Flower Among Thorns	3
Innocence in a World of Corruption	3
The Call of Purity	8
Refusing the Wealth of the World	11
Strength in Faith: Lessons for Modern Readers.	15
TEMPTATION AND TRIUMPH: The Test of Faith	19
The Threat of Persecution	19
Spiritual Warfare: The Battle for Purity	24
Agnes Before the Governor	29
Perseverance in Persecution	34
MIRACLES OF DEFIANCE: Protected By God's Grace	39
Agnes and the Fire	39
The Conversion of Witnesses	43
The Power of Witness: Martyrdom as a Catalyst	46
God's Grace in Modern Life	49
THE FINAL STAND: A Crown Of Martyrdom	53
The Execution Order	53
Agnes' Last Prayer	56
Martyrdom as Victory	59
Martyrs Today: The Call to Courage	62
AFTERMATH: The Legacy of St. Agnes	65
The Immediate Impact of Her Death	65
The Power of Her Relics	68
Building a Legacy: The Basilica of St. Agnes	71

Saints and Legacy: What Will We Leave Behind?	74
AGNES' INFLUENCE ACROSS THE AGES	77
Medieval Devotion to St. Agnes	77
Artists and Poets: Depictions of a Saint	80
Patroness of the Pure	83
Agnes in Our Times	85
ST. AGNES AND THE LAMB: Symbols Of Purity	88
The Symbol of the Lamb	88
Feast Day Traditions	91
Agnes as a Model of Sacrificial Love	93
Living Purity in a Corrupt World	96
LESSONS FROM ST. AGNES FOR TODAY'S CHRISTIAN	100
Purity of Heart in a Secular Society	100
Courage in the Face of Persecution	105
The Role of Women in the Church	109
Embracing the Cross with Joy	114

Introduction

A Journey Through Light and Shadow

In the heart of ancient Rome, among the grandeur of empire and the whispers of power, a flower of amazing purity bloomed. Her name was Agnes, and she was a beacon of faith and an embodiment of divine grace in a world on the verge of moral collapse. As we journey through St. Agnes' life, we will not only travel through historical corridors but also into the very soul of a young woman whose unwavering spirit and profound convictions transformed her into a symbol of triumph over tyranny, purity over corruption, and eternal light over fleeting shadows.

Consider a city where the magnificence of pagan temples dominates every street and cultural standards necessitate the surrender of personal convictions for the sake of power and status. Agnes, a wealthy and privileged child, opted to defy the odds in this turbulent environment. From the moment she heard Christ's call, her heart was fire with a zeal that would challenge the mightiest of empires and the most daunting of tribulations. Her journey is more than simply one girl's persistent determination; it is also a powerful monument to faith's transformational power.

In the pages that follow, we will see the sparkling clarity of her convictions as she rejects worldly allurements, her brave confrontation with the darkest forces of her day, and the supernatural protection that confirmed her sacred purpose. We shall travel with her through the fires of persecution, see the miraculous events that protected her, and comprehend the profundity of her final prayers, which will reverberate throughout the ages as a thundering monument to the triumph of spirit over flesh.

St. Agnes' story unfolds as a brilliant tapestry of light and shade, a dramatic narrative that spans time and space. Her life, defined by purity and sacrifice, is a compelling call to everyone who wants to know the genuine meaning of courage, faith, and divine grace. As we read through the chapters of her life, we will find ourselves reflecting on our own travels, motivated to embrace our crosses with the same pleasure and unshakeable faith that distinguished Agnes' life.

A story that combines historical depth with spiritual understanding, infusing each moment of struggle and triumph with the eternal power of divine love will enthrall you. This is more than just a biography of a saint; it is an invitation to delve deeply into what it means to live with unwavering faith in a challenging world. As you read these pages, allow the narrative of St. Agnes to inspire, challenge, and transform you, as it has done for countless others throughout history.

Welcome to a voyage of purity, power, and persecution—one that will enlighten the path of faith with the light of one of Christianity's most brilliant saints.

THE EARLY YEARS: A Flower Among Thorns

Innocence in a World of Corruption

Agnes, a child of noble descent, was born into a world of power and privilege in the heart of the Roman Empire. Her affluent and respected family moved in the greatest social circles, surrounded by Imperial Rome's magnificence. The palaces, temples, and marketplaces served as emblems of a powerful society whose influence extended throughout the known world. Agnes was exposed to the grandeur and magnificence that came with her family's wealth from a young age. Her upbringing was saturated with the sights and sounds of Roman aristocracy—banquets, rites, and gatherings that celebrated the empire's might and the gods who, according to Roman mythology, bestowed that authority. But beneath the splendor, a harsher reality remained.

Despite its wealth and power, Rome was a corrupt society. Agnes was born into a culture that was morally decaying. The civilization was dominated by pagan rituals, with citizens worshipping a pantheon of gods, offering sacrifices to idols, and engaging in decadent societal excesses. The Roman aristocracy valued pleasure, power, and fortune over morality, and many led lives marked by sin and self-indulgence. In this environment, innocence was frequently interpreted as weakness, and purity was scorned or dismissed.

Agnes, on the other hand, appeared to be unique from a young age. While everyone around her sought worldly pursuits, Agnes' heart was fixed on something much more. She grew up surrounded by temptations yet remained unaffected by them. Her beauty, which was visible even as a child, drew attention, but Agnes, with her unearthly grace, appeared unconcerned about the praise. What struck me the most about Agnes was her spiritual purity rather than her physical beauty. Even as a little child, she exuded a stunning innocence that set her apart in a world full of moral compromise.

Though her family was wealthy and influential, Agnes' spiritual richness actually characterized her. She had a tremendous commitment to Christ at an early age, and it appeared to grow deeper with each passing day. While the rest of Roman society worshipped pagan gods, Agnes modestly but steadfastly worshiped the one true God. She was initiated to Christianity while it was still considered a prohibited religion in the Roman Empire. Christianity, while flourishing, was not tolerated by the rulers, and those who practiced it faced persecution and death. Nonetheless, Agnes, even as a child, was unafraid. She embraced Christ's teachings with a pure heart and steadfast faith, a faith that would shape the rest of her life.

Despite their noble status, her family was not immune to the mounting conflicts between the pagan Roman world and the Christian faith. They were aware of the risks associated with following Christ, particularly for someone as young and vulnerable as Agnes. However, her devotion could not be contained. At a young age, Agnes demonstrated spiritual maturity beyond her years. She was drawn to prayer, frequently retreating into peaceful thought to spend hours in connection with God. She was noted for her kindness, gentleness, and persistent devotion to living a life consistent with Christ's teachings.

This deep commitment was not unnoticed. Even as a toddler, Agnes inspired many around her, particularly the little Christian community in Rome. Her innocence, rather than being a weakness, became a tremendous tribute to the strength of her faith. In a world where power and pleasure were paramount, Agnes stood as a silent rebuke to the depravity that was around her. She lived her life in a way that reflected the beauty of holiness, and her entire presence exuded an undeniable feeling of calm and purity.

Agnes's troubles increased as she developed. The pressures of the pagan world were consistent. The Roman aristocracy, in which her family held a respected position, provided numerous prospects for riches, power, and influence. Many young women of her age were groomed for marriages that would cement alliances and advance their families' wealth.

. Suitors from significant families would frequently want to marry daughters of nobility, ensuring that their own rank and money were reinforced by such marriages. For a girl like Agnes, recognized for her beauty and high standing, the expectations were clear: she would be courted by Rome's wealthiest and most powerful men, and her future would be one of opulence and social significance.

But, despite her youth, Agnes saw her future differently. Unlike her peers, she was not persuaded by the attraction of material wealth or the chance of an influential marriage. She had taken a sacred vow of virginity at a young age, committing her body and soul to Christ alone. This decision, taken with complete conviction, distinguished her even further. To the outside world, particularly those schooled in Roman norms, such a decision appeared incomprehensible, possibly even foolish. Why would a girl of such promise and beauty reject suitors who could provide her with wealth, power, and security? However, Agnes' heart was fixed on something far more eternal than worldly pleasures.

Her love for Christ served as her foundation. It was not a casual belief, nor did she express it casually. Her bond with her Savior was profound and abiding, and it guided every area of her life. The simplicity and purity with which she lived reflected her soul's wish to be free of the world's influences. Agnes recognized that the treasures of this world were fleeting, compared to the glory of eternity with God. For her, marriage, no matter how great or wonderful, paled in contrast to the relationship she desired with Christ.

This decision, however, would not be without problems. As Agnes entered adolescence, the urge to adhere to societal expectations increased. Suitors arrived, each more powerful and affluent than the last, anxious to have Mary as their bride. Among them was the son of a Roman prefect, a man with considerable power in the empire. He had heard of Agnes' beauty and purity, and, like many others, he was attracted by the prospect of marrying her. His family, which was well-connected and influential, regarded the marriage as an opportunity to expand their authority. However, Agnes considered such a union unthinkable. She had already surrendered her heart to Christ, and no earthly man could replace Him.

When Agnes rejected his approaches, the young suitor was perplexed and outraged. In a world when women were frequently viewed as possessions or status symbols, the idea of someone declining such an offer seemed inconceivable. Agnes' refusal, however, was solid and steadfast. Nothing could break her promise to God, regardless of wealth, power, or influence. The young man, offended by her refusal, became enraged, and what began as a harmless pursuit of her hand suddenly developed into something far more serious.

Agnes' rejection of the prefect's son set off a chain of events that would finally lead to her arrest. Despite rising threats, she remained firm. Her innocence, rather than protecting her from the horrors of the world, appeared to make her a more vulnerable victim. In a society that valued strength, power, and dominance, Agnes' purity was interpreted as a rebellion against Rome's core principles. Her decision to live a chaste life committed only to Christ was not just a personal commitment but also a public declaration that she belonged to a different kingdom—a heavenly one that contrasted sharply with the empire in which she lived.

Despite her youth, Agnes was aware of the risks. She understood that following Christ comes with a price, and in her case, that cost could be her life. Nonetheless, she did not waver. Her heart was filled with the calm that comes from knowing she was following God's plan. In a corrupt world, she was like a flower blooming among the thorns, unaffected by the immorality around her.

Agnes' innocence and strong commitment to Christ would continue to characterize her life, even as Rome's soldiers closed in on her. The demands of the pagan world, the temptation of wealth and rank, and threats from those in authority would all work to weaken her resolve. But Agnes, filled with faith, stood firm, knowing that her purity was more than just a physical state; it was a sign of her unwavering devotion to her Savior.

Her brief existence would serve as a strong message to the world, demonstrating that innocence and purity, when founded in Christ, can survive even the darkest of forces. As Agnes grew older, her faith journey deepened, and her devotion to Christ shone even greater in the face of persecution.

The Call of Purity

As Agnes developed into adolescence, her pledge of chastity became more than just a personal act of devotion; it was a strong statement of her identity in a world that prized power, wealth, and pleasure above all else. In Roman culture, a woman's worth was frequently determined by the alliances she could form through marriage and the influence she could have over her family. For a girl of Agnes' noble upbringing and dazzling beauty, her destiny was predetermined—she was expected to marry into riches and power, elevating her family's status in the empire. But Agnes had taken a different path, one that was directly opposed to the norms of her period.

Her decision to take the vow of chastity was not taken lightly. Agnes had a profound and intimate relationship with Christ since she was a child—a love so great that she could not conceive sharing her heart or body with anyone else. This pledge reflected her distinct devotion to God, which she adored and zealously defended. For Agnes, purity was more than just a physical state; it was a spiritual vocation, a road that demanded fortitude, tenacity, and unflinching faith in God's will for her life.

In a culture where a woman's fate was frequently determined by her family and cultural expectations, Agnes' pledge of chastity was regarded as both uncommon and perplexing. Marriage was more than just a personal decision; it was a social and political arrangement, particularly among the nobility. Young ladies of noble blood were frequently groomed from an early age to attract the most powerful and prominent suitors, and a family's success was often dependent on finding favorable marriages. Refusing such suitors meant not only defying cultural norms but also rejecting Roman life's very underpinnings.

However, Agnes saw the call to purity as a higher calling that went beyond her family's and society's expectations. Her heart was focused on Christ alone, and she pledged to be His wife for all eternity. This decision, albeit intensely personal, had public consequences. According to Roman society, Agnes' vow represented a rejection of everything they loved. The powerful men who sought her hand in marriage saw her denial as an insult, a defiance of their authority and influence. And in a world where power meant everything, such rebellion was not readily forgiven.

Agnes endured enormous hurdles. Suitors, many of whom were prominent and influential, approached her family, wanting her to be their wife. They were lured not only to her beauty but also to her great heritage, knowing that marrying Agnes would provide them with prestige and influence. Among them was the son of the Roman prefect, a man whose influence extended to the highest levels of the empire. He had heard about Agnes' beauty and morality, and he was determined to win her hand. His family, too, saw the merger as a strategic relationship that would help them advance even farther.

But Agnes stayed steadfast. When the prefect's son approached her with a proposition of wealth, power, and the security of a prestigious marriage, Agnes politely and firmly declined. She had already pledged herself to Christ; she continued, and no worldly marriage could compare to her relationship with her Savior. Her rejection was not one of disdain or arrogance but of deep devotion. However, to the suitor, her remarks were incomprehensible. He could not comprehend why any woman, especially one of such beauty and status, would forego a life of luxury and power in favor of an invisible God.

As news of Agnes' refusal spread, so did the scorn and disbelief. Many people found her decision not just perplexing but also highly offensive. In Roman society, a woman who refused marriage and the position given to her was regarded with suspicion. Rejecting a strong man's advances was an affront to his honor and a violation of societal norms. Agnes had accomplished both by opting for a pure lifestyle. Her decision put her in a difficult situation, both socially and politically. The more she fought the pressures of the world around her, the worse her predicament became.

The prefect's kid was hurt by her refusal and did not take it well. His pride had been harmed, and in Roman society where power was everything, such an insult could not go unnoticed. He, like others before him, had assumed that his wealth, influence, and charm would be enough to win Agnes' hand. When these failed, his admiration evolved into rage. How could a thirteen-year-old girl hold steady against big men's desires? How could she refuse something that every other woman in her position would have accepted without hesitation?

But Agnes was unlike other ladies. Her strength came from her unshakeable faith in Christ, not the power of her family or her beauty. She knew the world would never comprehend her decision, but she also knew she could not break her pledge to God. For Mary, the call to purity was more than just a personal virtue; it was a profound expression of her devotion to Christ. She had chosen to devote her life to Him, and no earthly temptation could persuade her from that decision.

Agnes' rejection of the prefect's son would have repercussions. His rage, fueled by pride and a sense of entitlement, would set in motion a chain of events that would result in her being persecuted. Despite the mounting pressures and threats against her, Agnes maintained her dedication. She understood that her purity, her vow of virginity, was a gift she had made to Christ, and no earthly power could take it away from her.

Agnes saw the call to purity as a summons to live a special life. In a world when power, rank, and fortune were valued above all else, Agnes took a different path—one of humility, devotion, and unshakeable faith. Her virginity was more than just a rejection of worldly ideals; it was a powerful testament to God's love. It was a declaration that true strength came not from wealth or influence but from a heart completely devoted to Jesus.

THE EARLY YEARS: A FLOWER AMONG THORNS

Refusing the Wealth of the World

The day Agnes was presented with one of her most prominent suitors began like any other in her young life, yet the enormity of the occasion hung heavy in the air. Her father had mentioned the meeting the night before, his tone official and tight, aware that this particular request could change the path of their family's destiny. The suitor, the son of a Roman prefect, was a man of enormous power and fortune, and his interest in Agnes was more than just personal passion; it was a calculated maneuver that promised to propel both families to new heights of dominance.

Marriages in Roman society were rarely based on love. They were partnerships formed to protect power, riches, and social status. A marriage to such a man would have provided Agnes with a life of luxury, stability, and renown. But Agnes, despite being well aware of the demands put on her, knew deep down that this suitor, like all those before him, would never be able to provide her with what she truly sought. Her heart belonged only to Christ, and no earthly offer, no matter how rich, could dissuade her from her commitment.

When the big day arrived, Agnes prepared herself not with the joy or nervous expectation of a girl waiting for a proposal but with the quiet strength of someone ready to defend her beliefs. The suitor came to her family's villa with a spectacular parade, his chariot gleaming in the bright Roman sun. His appearance was a spectacle, with servants in rich clothes, gifts of gold and valuable stones, and a retinue of noblemen standing as witnesses to the momentous alliance he hoped to seal. His wealth was visible in every aspect, from the silks he wore to the extravagant gifts he carried, each meticulously selected to impress and captivate.

However, Agnes greeted him with the quiet elegance that had always distinguished her. Her beauty was evident, even when she was dressed simply, but what impressed those in attendance was her calm, unshakable manner. She was only thirteen years old, but she held herself with the grace and poise of someone much older, as if her previous struggles had purified her character.

The suitor, who was used to women falling at his feet, was instantly fascinated by her beauty. He approached her with confidence, his voice smooth and rehearsed, and spoke words of praise and admiration. He talked about their luxurious, influential life together, where she would have everything. He promised her estates, jewelry, and the finest clothing. He told her that her future would be one of comfort and ease, with servants attending to all of her needs and her name being spoken with respect and admiration throughout the empire.

But as he spoke, Agnes sensed a growing sensation of distance from the reality he depicted. The riches and power that others sought appeared hollow to her. She listened respectfully, her heart stable and her mind fixed on Christ, the only true love in her life. When the suitor ended his statement, expecting at least a gleam of approval from Agnes, she sat silent for a time, gathering her thoughts and hoping for the courage to respond with grace and sincerity.

When she finally spoke, her tone was quiet yet forceful.
"I thank you for the honor of your proposal," she began calmly.
"but I cannot accept what you offer." Her rejection was calm, almost compassionate, yet it held the weight of her unwavering conviction. She looked at him straight, her eyes shining with the light of her conviction.
"I have already given myself to another,
" she explained. "My heart belongs to Christ, and I have vowed to remain pure for Him alone."

Her comments landed like stones in a quiet pond, eliciting shock and disbelief. The suitor, who was unaccustomed to rejection, particularly from someone so young, blinked in surprise. He had expected flattery, possibly even a bashful acceptance, but not this. The idea of a young girl rejecting money and power in favor of an invisible God was strange to him, as it was to the majority of Roman society. He looked to her father, expecting him to intervene and correct what was clearly a misunderstanding. But Agnes' father, torn between his love for his daughter and societal standards, remained silent, knowing that Agnes' decision in this issue could not be overturned.

However, the suitor was not one to give up easy. He pressed on, his tone becoming more forceful. "You do not understand what you are refusing," he replied, his voice tinged with displeasure. "I can provide you with unlimited wealth, status, and influence. "You will be a queen among women." He moved closer, lowering his voice as if chatting confidentially with her. "Imagine what your life could be like with me," Agnes says. "All of Rome will envy you."

But Agnes was unconvinced. Her gaze was unwavering, and her heart was grounded in her conviction about her decision. "I do understand," she said, her voice steady.
"You offer me the riches of this world, but I want the treasures of heaven. You promise me a life of luxury, but I have already chosen purity and dedication to Christ. "No power on Earth can change that."

Her comments, uttered without rage, struck the suitor like a blow. His pride shattered; he took a step back, his cheeks flushed with frustration. This was not how the interaction was supposed to unfold. He had come anticipating praise, perhaps even appreciation, but instead he was met by a little girl who spoke with the power and conviction of someone far older than her years.

"Do you know who I am?" he questioned, his tone tinted with rage. "Are you aware of the power I possess? I could make your life really difficult, Agnes. Do not assume that your refusal will go unnoticed.

Agnes met his gaze with fearlessness. "I fear only one," she replied gently, "and that is not you." My loyalty is to Christ, and I will not betray Him, no matter what the cost.

The suitor, now outraged, turned to her father and demanded that he interfere, forcing his daughter to see sense. Her father, though visibly concerned, recognized that Agnes' mind was made up. He, too, had realized that her dedication to Christ was unshakeable.

In the days that followed, the suitor's rage only intensified. His rejection by Agnes, a mere girl, humiliated him, and he promised that she would come to regret her decision. He circulated news of her refusal in the hopes of damaging her reputation, but instead, the story of her faith and courage spread across Rome's Christian community. What the suitor perceived as an insult, others recognized as a demonstration of Agnes' commitment to Christ.

For Agnes, the experience was just one of many trials, but it strengthened her resolve. She was unaffected by the world's money and power. She had chosen Christ, the road to eternal glory. Her heart remained pure, and her soul was unaffected by the temptations that so easily enticed others. In rejecting the suitor, Agnes not only kept her pledge, but she declared to all who would listen that her life belonged solely to God.

THE EARLY YEARS: A FLOWER AMONG THORNS

Strength in Faith: Lessons for Modern Readers.

Agnes' unwavering devotion to her faith is more than just a remnant of old history; it is a strong and timeless lesson for modern Christians, particularly the young. At a time when society expects people, particularly young people, to conform to popular ideals of success, wealth, and power, Agnes' decision to follow Christ above all serves as a reminder that true strength is found not in external accomplishments but in an unwavering commitment to what is right and true. Her life exemplifies the immense power of faith, which transcends time, society, and situation.

Many young Christians today suffer pressures that can be equally intense, even if they do not receive marriage proposals from Roman nobility. The world today, like Agnes' day, frequently prioritizes financial prosperity, social prestige, and physical appearance over spiritual depth and personal integrity. Young people are continually assaulted with signals that their worth is determined by what they can accomplish, how they appear, and how many people follow them on social media. In this environment, remaining true to one's faith can appear difficult, if not impossible.

Agnes faced demands similar to those of today: conform to the world's values or risk being excluded. Nonetheless, she refused to succumb to those pressures, even at the expense of her safety and status. She recognized that her worth was defined by her connection with Christ rather than by societal standards. Her tale is a remarkable example for modern readers, particularly young Christians, of the freedom that comes from knowing that your identity is anchored in something unchanging and eternal. Agnes' heart was securely anchored in her religion; thus, she was unmoved by the ephemeral joys of wealth or men's approval.

One of the most significant lessons from Agnes' life is that faith, when cultivated in childhood, may become a rock-solid basis for the future. Her resolve to stay chaste and devoted to Christ came when she was just thirteen, a time of great doubt and self-discovery. However, Agnes knew who she was and, more importantly, whose she was. Her clarity of purpose, especially at such a young age, exemplifies the importance of early spiritual formation. For parents, teachers, and mentors, her narrative emphasizes the significance of imparting strong values and a profound relationship to Christ in children from a young age.

In today's fast-paced society, young people are frequently urged to prioritize their careers, personal goals, and future accomplishments, sometimes at the price of their spiritual life. However, Agnes' narrative defies that view. It demonstrates that the most important decisions a person may make are not about which college to attend, what job path to pursue, or even whom to marry, but about where their heart and soul are grounded. Agnes considered everything else to be secondary to her relationship with Christ. Her decision to remain faithful in the face of enormous pressure exemplifies the immense power that comes from placing one's religion over all else.

Agnes' story also displays how faith may provide strength in the face of adversity. When the powerful suitor threatened her with retaliation, she refused to back down or compromise. Her strength stemmed not from any earthly power but from her unwavering faith in God. In a society where young people frequently feel powerless in the face of cultural expectations, Agnes' tale provides hope. It demonstrates that true strength stems from holding firm in one's convictions, even when it is difficult.

Her faith was more than a comfort in times of trouble; it was her foundation. For modern readers, this is an important point. Faith is not a last resort when things go wrong, but rather a way of life that influences every decision, action, and connection. Agnes' tale serves as a reminder that faith must be nurtured on a daily basis via prayer, thought, and a dedication to following Christ's teachings. This type of faith provides the resilience to face the hardships that life inevitably presents.

Furthermore, Agnes' purity was more than simply physical chastity; it also included maintaining the purity of her heart, mind, and spirit. In today's world, where distractions and temptations abound, young Christians might find inspiration in Agnes' commitment to maintaining her inner purity. She guarded her heart tightly, not out of fear but out of her love for Christ. Her reluctance to compromise, even when under enormous pressure, demonstrates that real purity is more than just saying no to the wrong things; it is also about saying yes to the right things—most notably, to a Christ-centered life.

Agnes' story also teaches us that sticking to religion frequently requires fortitude and the willingness to stand out from the crowd. Her unwillingness to comply with Roman society's standards was a radical move, involving substantial personal risk. She did not hesitate, though, since she knew her reward would be in the next world, not this one. Agnes' story serves as a striking message to today's young Christians, who may feel alone or even mocked because of their convictions. By remaining true to their faith, they are following in the footsteps of many saints who have come before them, taking strength from the same God who sustained Agnes during her time of need.

Modern readers are encouraged to contemplate their own faith journeys as they reflect on Agnes' faith strength. In what aspects of their lives do they feel pressured to adhere to global standards? Where are they being asked to remain firm, even if it means standing alone? Agnes' example urges young Christians to review their priorities and consider whether they are living for the world's ephemeral rewards or for Christ's eternal promises.

Agnes' narrative also inspires us to believe in God's purpose, even if it appears tough or obscure. Her path was not easy, and she was rejected, isolated, and persecuted because of her religion. Nonetheless, she believed that God's plan for her was superior to anything the world could provide. This is a message that connects strongly with today's youth, many of whom are seeking meaning and direction in an uncertain world. Agnes' story demonstrates that, even in the midst of uncertainty, we can be confident that God is with us, guiding us, and that our faith will be rewarded in ways we cannot always see.

As young Christians ponder on Agnes' experience, they are encouraged to explore how they, too, might lead lives of unshakeable faith. In a world that frequently requires compromise, Agnes' life is a bright example of the beauty and power of remaining loyal to one's values. Her courage, purity, and deep love for Christ are timeless lessons for those who strive to walk the path of faith.

Agnes' faith is a shining example for young Christians today, demonstrating that no matter what challenges or temptations they experience, they, too, may remain steadfast in their love for Christ. Her life serves as a reminder that true power is found not in worldly prosperity but in a heart completely devoted to God.

TEMPTATION AND TRIUMPH: The Test of Faith

The Threat of Persecution

Rome, long a bastion of unrivaled power and culture, had become a source of rising concern for Christians such as Agnes. The emperor ordered the empire to accept only its faith. Christians were regarded as disruptive because their refusal to worship the Roman gods represented a direct challenge to the emperor's authority. However, for Agnes, this threat paled in comparison to the deeper conflict she felt within herself—the desire to succumb to fear, to compromise her beliefs in order to survive.

Agnes understood the stakes. The Roman authorities had started deliberately persecuting Christians, demanding public allegiance to the emperor and the pagan gods. Those who rejected were subjected to harsh punishment, even death. As whispers of new edicts spread through the streets, families like hers lived in continual anxiety. The sword of persecution hung above their heads, but Agnes was more concerned with whether her religion would withstand strain than with pain or death.

It was not long before she received direct threats of persecution. Agnes was noted not only for her beauty and purity but also for her strong and unwavering Christian faith. Her refusal to accept the suitor's marriage proposal had already put her on the radar of the city's influential men, and her subsequent rejection of wealth and rank in favor of her dedication to Christ had only fueled their desire to see her broken. Word had spread that she was not like other girls; she could not be swayed by the typical promises of wealth, power, and luxury.

For the Roman rulers, such rebellion was risky. A young girl with such strong convictions constituted a severe threat to the order they intended to maintain. If Agnes could refuse and resist the world's attractions, others could follow. Her influence, however modest, posed a danger to the empire's power. The message needed to be clear: no one defies Rome without consequences.

The day they arrived, Agnes was praying in a small, private chapel within her family's villa. It was a refuge, a place where she could escape the world's clamor and focus on God's presence. As she knelt in stillness, she could feel the weight of her decision crushing against her. She had chosen Christ above all else, and now the time for testing had arrived. Will her faith be intact when faced with the full might of Roman authority?

The sound of footsteps echoed down the hall, becoming louder and more intense. A troop of Roman soldiers had arrived at the estate, led by an official notorious for harshly enforcing the Emperor's edicts. The doors swung open, and Agnes' parents ran to greet them, their faces blanched with fright. They understood why the soldiers had arrived. They had been dreading this day since news of Christian persecution spread. Their innocent daughter, Agnes, had become the target of Rome's merciless crusade against the faithful.

TEMPTATION AND TRIUMPH: THE TEST OF FAITH

Agnes, however, remained composed. She stepped up from her posture of devotion, her expression peaceful, as if she had been anticipating this moment all along. In fact, she had. Agnes knew from the moment she fully pledged her life to Christ that her faith would be tested in ways she could not have imagined. The Roman world demanded complete fidelity, leaving Christians with only two options: abandon Christ or risk punishment.

The Roman official, Quintianus, entered the chamber with authority, examining the space before focusing on Agnes. He had heard of her—this young girl who had turned down a prominent suitor and shunned the attraction of wealth and rank. To him, she was an outlier, a curiosity. He believed she could be persuaded to see reason. After all, she was still a child, and like all children, she might be convinced.

"Agnes," he murmured, his voice silky yet authoritative. "You are called to appear before the magistrate. There is a matter of great importance that must be addressed."

Agnes stared at him, her expression steadfast. She understood what he meant. She, like so many others before her, would be required to publicly declare her loyalty to the Emperor and provide a sacrifice to the Roman gods. It was a test aimed at shattering Christians' will by forcing them to abandon their faith in exchange for their lives.

"I will come," Agnes murmured gently, coming forward with confidence that belied her youth. Her parents, standing behind her, were terrified, but they knew their daughter too well to attempt to stop her. They had raised her in faith and nurtured her love for Christ, and all they could do now was hope that God would give her the strength she needed to face what lay ahead.

The soldiers led her through the streets of Rome, and the atmosphere was tense. People stared from their doors and windows, some with sympathy in their eyes, others with sick fascination. It was not every day that a little girl was brought before the power of Roman authority, and the audience muttered with pity and doubt. What might happen to her? Would she succumb? Could a young girl possibly have the bravery to challenge the world's most powerful empire?

Agnes, for her part, stayed silent. Her heart was solid, and her thoughts were focused on Christ. She had made her decision long ago, and as the moment of confrontation approached, she felt a tremendous peace settle within her. She understood what was at stake—her life and freedom—but she also knew that no earthly power could take away the love and salvation she had found in Christ.

When they arrived at the magistrate's court, the scene had already been set. The room was packed with Roman officials, troops, and interested bystanders. At the middle of it all sat the magistrate, a man renowned for strict adherence to the emperor's edicts. He glanced down at Agnes with disdain and bemusement. What could a girl like her expect to gain by rejecting the empire?

"Agnes," the magistrate started, his voice resonating throughout the chamber. "You stand accused of defying the emperor's will; it is said that you refuse to worship Rome's gods and instead pledge your allegiance to the one you call Christ." He paused, allowing the severity of the situation to set in. "Is this true?"

Agnes stood before him with her head held high. "Yes," she answered, her voice firm and unwavering. "I worship Christ alone, the true and living God."

The room went silent. The magistrate raised an eyebrow, evidently not anticipating such audacity. He leaned forward, his tone becoming more sinister. "You understand, of course, what this means. To refuse Rome's gods is to refuse the emperor himself. You must abandon this so-called Christ and make a sacrifice to the gods. Do so, and you will be spared. Refuse, and you will face the consequences."

For a little while, the weight of the decision hovered in the air. Agnes understood that rejecting Christ would save her from imminent death. She could walk away, return to her family, and enjoy a life of comfort. All she had to do was make a small sacrifice and say a few words of devotion to the emperor, and everything would be over. The desire to succumb, to rescue herself, had to have been overwhelming. However, Agnes understood in her heart that abandoning Christ at that time meant losing everything that truly mattered.

"I cannot," Agnes murmured gently, her voice full of quiet determination. "I belong to Christ. I will not betray Him."

The magistrate's face clouded. "Do you truly understand what you are refusing?" he said with anger. "You are but a child, and yet you throw away your life for the sake of a dead man?"

Agnes' eyes met his, revealing the power of her trust. "He is not dead," she explained. "He lives, and I live with him."

The magistrate's patience had become thin. He slapped his hand on the table in front of him, his voice rising in wrath. "Then you've chosen your fate! You will be punished for your defiance. Take her away!"

The troops approached her, but Agnes did not resist. As they escorted her out of the courtroom, she felt a profound feeling of calm, knowing that she had remained faithful to Christ even in the face of death. Her desire to save herself had been tremendous, but her love for Christ was stronger.

Agnes faced even greater challenges in the days that followed, yet her faith remained unwavering. She had chosen the path of suffering not because she desired martyrdom but because her love for Christ outweighed all the world's temptations. For modern readers, Agnes' confrontation with the Roman authorities is a poignant reminder that profound faith can survive even the most extreme threats and temptations.

Spiritual Warfare: The Battle for Purity

Agnes sat in the cold, dark cell, her physical surroundings reflecting her internal spiritual struggle. The prison's silence was stifling, broken only by the distant noises of guards shifting in their places and the occasional cries of other detainees. Although this isolation provided a respite from the noise and bustle of the outside world, it also brought with it an even deeper challenge. Agnes would face her most difficult battle here, alone with her thoughts: the war for purity, not only in body but also in mind and spirit.

Agnes understood that her war was more than just against the Roman rulers and the bodily tortures they threatened. It was a much deeper fight on the spiritual battlefield. The forces of evil attempted to erode her determination, sowing seeds of doubt, fear, and despair. As the young girl sat in the damp confines of her cell, the temptations she had encountered from powerful men outside were insignificant in comparison to the whispers of fear and uncertainty that now filled her head.

Is her suffering worthwhile? Was her constancy foolish? These were the questions that started to sneak in. Despite her uncertainties, she heard another, stronger voice—the voice of her faith—reminding her that her purity and dedication were for Christ, not the world. The world gave her wealth, marriage, rank, and freedom—everything a young Roman woman could want. But Agnes had chosen a different road, one that led to eternal promises in heaven rather than the transient joys of this life.

Nonetheless, the internal conflict was unrelenting. Agnes was human, after all, and she felt the weight of what lay ahead of her. Her flesh shivered at the prospect of the tortures that were ahead of her, and she was terrified of what she would face. She would hear stories about Christians who had been thrown to wild beasts, burned at the stake, or worse. The fear of suffering, the inherent impulse to protect her own life, tugged at her heart. Could she really bear such pain and remain faithful? In the face of excruciating agony, would her strength hold up?

In this moment of deep vulnerability, Agnes turned to prayer, her most potent weapon in the spiritual struggle. Kneeling on the cold stone floor of her cell, she lifted her heart to God, seeking the strength that He alone could supply. Her prayer words came from the depths of her soul, rather than her lips.

"Lord, give me strength," she said quietly, her voice shaking but honest. "You know my heart. You know my fear. However, you are greater than any fear that threatens me. Let Your will be done in me. Let me remain pure in body and in spirit, for I am Yours."

Agnes sensed a presence in the prison's silence, a tranquility that enveloped her like a blanket of light. It was the presence of Christ, her bridegroom, to whom she had pledged her life and purity. In that moment, Agnes realized she was not fighting alone. Her virginity and chastity were not something she could defend on her own; they were a gift, a treasure that Christ Himself guarded. Her war was not fought alone; Christ stood beside her, strengthening her through His grace.

Her struggle for purity, especially in such a hostile environment, went beyond bodily chastity, though that was important. It was about staying true to her identity as a daughter of God, even while the world around her tried to take it away. The Roman authorities, as well as the suitors who desired her hand, were solely interested in her outer beauty, innocence, and prospects for marriage and motherhood. However, Agnes understood that these things did not define her worth. Her ultimate beauty was found in her steadfast faith, her soul's devotion to Christ.

As she prayed, Agnes was reminded of the numerous saints who had come before her, people who had experienced persecution but remained true to their faith. Her head was filled with the legends of martyrs such as St. Cecilia and St. Lucy, providing her with both consolation and strength. These women, like her, were lured, tortured, and intimidated. They had been promised every possible worldly benefit in exchange for their faith, but they had chosen Christ above all else. Agnes believed that the same strength that had gotten them through their tribulations would also help her.

However, the battle for purity extended beyond the exterior forces of temptation and terror. It was also a war against pride. The temptation to believe that she could get through these hardships on her own power was subtle but perilous. Agnes understood that pride, like fear, might take her away from Christ. She could not rely just on her willpower and commitment. Her innocence—her very life—belonged to Christ, and He alone would bring her through the storm.

In this spiritual battle, Agnes faced not only the exterior demands of Rome but also internal temptations that aimed to undermine her faith. The desire to succumb to fear, to take a simpler route, to escape suffering at all costs, pressed on her heart. But as these temptations increased, so did her reliance on prayer and God's love. She found strength in entrusting her fear, doubts, and even her life to the one who had already triumphed over sin and death.

Agnes' quest for purity mirrored the difficulty that all Christians confront in their spiritual lives. Whether it is the temptation to conform to the world, compromise on beliefs, or allow fear to drive decisions, every Christian is challenged to fight this struggle at some point. Agnes, despite her early age, knew this completely. Her refusal to marry and her rejection of wealth and power were more than just personal choices; they were acts of resistance against the corrupt principles of the world around her. They were assertions of her identity as God's chosen child, set apart for His purposes.

Agnes found light in the darkness of her cell, knowing that her bodily and spiritual purity could not be taken away via force. The Roman authorities could arrest, torment, and even kill her, but they could not touch the purity of her soul. That was something she freely gave to Christ, and it was now in His hands alone.

As the hours turned into days and the prospect of torture became more real, Agnes' faith grew stronger. Her complete reliance on God enabled her to win the inner battle for purity and perseverance. The fear of pain and suffering was still present, but it no longer controlled her. Agnes had chosen her path, and no matter what the Roman authorities did, they could not sever the relationship she shared with her Lord.

For modern readers, Agnes' spiritual warfare offers a powerful illustration of what it means to live a pure life in a world that frequently rewards the reverse. Her narrative is not only about a girl who denied marriage or fortune but also about a soul who refused to sacrifice her core principles, even in the face of death. In a society where purity, in all its forms, is sometimes ignored or undervalued, Agnes stands out as a light of hope and courage, reminding us that true purity is more than simply physical chastity; it is also about living a life completely dedicated to God.

Agnes Before the Governor

Agnes stood in the magnificent hall of the governor's palace, her petite form overwhelmed by the room's luxury and power. The marble floors sparkled under her bare feet, cold and harsh, in sharp contrast to the soft warmth of her childhood home. Golden tapestries adorned the walls, showing the Roman gods in all their glory, a striking tribute to the empire's wealth and might. Soldiers stood in position along the walls, their armor clanking as they shuffled uncomfortably. Governor Aspasius sat before her on an elevated platform, his demeanor mysterious but his power apparent. Advisors, scribes, and spectators surrounded him, waiting to witness the death of another Christian victim.

But Agnes was unlike the others. Her bravery was well beyond her years, despite the fact that she was barely out of childhood. She stood upright, her face placid, her gaze concentrated not on the governor or the troops but beyond them, as if she saw something much larger than the trial she was about to face. She possessed a strength that unnerved those in the room. Her entire existence seemed to question the empire's authority—not through revolt or defiance, but through the serene assurance of faith.

Governor Aspasius looked at her with a mixture of wonder and frustration. He had seen countless Christians brought before him, cowering in terror or defiance, but this girl was unique. She was cool and composed, yet something about her made him nervous. She should have been scared; most people her age would have asked for mercy. But here she stood, a little girl, unconcerned by the gravity of the situation.

"Agnes," the governor started, his voice resounding through the hall, "you are accused of being a Christian, of refusing to worship the gods of Rome, and of rejecting the suitors who have sought your hand in marriage. Do you understand the consequences of your choices?"

Agnes gazed up at him, her expression sweet but determined. "I do," she answered, her voice firm and unwavering. "I have given my life to Christ, and I will not forsake Him. No power on this earth, no threat, can make me turn away from my Lord."

The crowd murmured in response to her words. Aspasius moved slightly forward, his face deepening. "Do you realize what you are saying?" he inquired, his voice becoming more furious. "You defy the laws of Rome. You insult the gods. You reject the empire's authority. And for what? For a faith in a man who died a criminal's death?"

Agnes met his stare, and her eyes shone with a brightness that seemed to blaze from inside. "He died, yes," she said sadly, "but He rose again. And He lives. I live for Him and Him alone."

The governor clinched his jaw. He had intended to argue with her, perhaps scare her into surrender, but this girl was immune to terror. He signaled to one of the guards, who stepped forward, clutching a bundle of exquisite textiles and jewels—the gifts bestowed by the suitors who sought her hand. The soldier set them in front of her, glistening in the torchlight.

"Look at what you are rejecting," Aspasius remarked, his tone softening as if to appeal to her sense of reason. "Wealth, status, comfort. You could be married to one of the most powerful men in Rome and live a life of luxury and ease. Why throw all of this away for a faith that will only bring you death?"

Agnes took in the wealth before her: gold and silk, diamonds and pearls. To any other girl her age, it would have been the ultimate temptation—an escape from suffering and a comfortable future. However, Agnes saw no worth in these things when contrasted to the eternal treasures she had discovered in Christ.

"I do not want these things," she stated gently. "I have already given my heart to the King of Kings. I am His bride, and no earthly riches can compare to the love I have in Him."

The governor's patience began to wear thin. He had no desire to harm a child, but her stubbornness gave him no choice. He understood the law, and it was apparent. If she refused to repent, her fate was sealed. He stood straight, casting a broad shadow over the room, and addressed her sternly.

"You have one last chance, Agnes. Denounce your faith, offer sacrifice to the gods, and you will walk free. Refuse, and you will face the full weight of Rome's justice."

As everyone turned their attention to Agnes, a heavy stillness fell over the room. The tension was apparent, and the air was thick with expectancy. However, Agnes, with her unshakeable faith, remained calm. She raised her eyes to the heavens, and the room appeared to change. A peculiar light flooded the room, mild at first and then increasing in intensity. The onlookers shifted uncomfortably, peering about in confusion.

"I will never abandon my Lord," she declared firmly. "No matter what you do to me, my soul belongs to Christ."

A sudden rush of wind swept through the hall as she spoke, despite the fact that the windows were locked and the night outside was calm. The torches flashed, and their flames danced furiously. And then something extraordinary occurred. As the governor opened his mouth to order the guards to seize her, the flame of the greatest torch in the room burst from its position and engulfed the mound of riches put before Agnes. The silks and gems burst into flames, burning them in an instant and converting the exquisite offerings to ash.

Gasps rang around the room as the crowd took a step back, shocked by the unexpected blaze. The governor's face darkened, and his eyes widened in surprise. Was this an act of the gods? Or was there something more? The individuals in the room began to speak among themselves, some discussing divine involvement and others wondering if the gods were displeased.

Agnes stood in the heart of it all, unaffected by the flames, her gaze still fixed on heaven. She realized this was not a coincidence. Christ was with her even in this time of suffering. He was her guardian and shield, and no worldly power could rob her of her faith.

Despite being shocked by the abrupt fire, Governor Aspasius was undeterred. He smashed his hand against the arm of his chair, his wrath bubbling over. "This is sorcery!" he exclaimed. "Take her to the place of shame. If she will not be swayed by riches, then we will break her spirit."

The soldiers paused for a while, confused by what they had just observed, but went forward on the governor's orders. They seized Agnes by the arms and started dragging her out of the hall. As they did so, the audience stood in stunned silence, some in admiration of her fortitude, others terrified of what might happen.

Agnes did not struggle as they brought her away. She walked with serene dignity, her gaze fixed forward, and her heart full of the awareness that Christ was with her. Though the governor had threatened her with disgrace, Agnes understood that no worldly humiliation could penetrate her soul. Her purity, faith, and devotion were all tied to Christ, and no power in Rome could take them away.

As the hall doors closed behind her, the governor leaned back in his chair, his mind spinning with uncertainty and anger. He had seen many challenges in his life, but nothing like this. This girl had a unique, otherworldly quality. He could not explain the fire or the unwavering courage she demonstrated. Nonetheless, he knew his role was obvious. Agnes had defied the law.

But as the night passed and the palace became quieter, the governor felt uneasy. In his quest to uphold the empire's laws, had he just convicted someone genuinely holy?

Perseverance in Persecution

Agnes' narrative of unshakable faith in the face of harsh persecution contains timeless lessons for Christians today. While we may not encounter physical difficulties like the early Christian martyrs, the essence of persecution can still be found in the spiritual, emotional, and social problems that believers face in a world that frequently contradicts the Gospel's principles. Agnes' tenacity, boldness, and unwavering dedication to Christ are powerful examples of how modern Christians can stay steadfast even when it appears that the entire world is against them.

In our fast-paced and materialistic environment, challenges to our religion are frequently subtle. They may not be as obvious as standing before a Roman governor or being carried to execution, yet they can be equally tough to bear. The pressure to adhere to society conventions and sacrifice our convictions in order to improve our careers, get social approval, or even maintain intimate relationships can be overpowering. Nonetheless, Agnes' narrative demonstrates that even in the face of enormous pressure, it is possible to remain committed to Christ.

Agnes' persecution was the direct result of her reluctance to abandon her faith in Christ and conform to the religious and cultural norms of her period. She was not persuaded by the attraction of wealth, status, or safety because she recognized something that all Christians must remember: our citizenship is not in this world, but in God's kingdom. When confronted with choices that test our faith, we must remember that what we stand for as Christians is far more important than the transitory joys or comforts that this world may provide.

One of the most important takeaways from Agnes' life is her sense of self.

She recognized who she was in Christ, which enabled her to be steadfast in her convictions. The world around her attempted to define her based on external criteria—her money, attractiveness, and suitability for marriage to a prominent suitor. But Agnes had already made her decision. Her life belonged to Christ, and this commitment influenced every action, response, and stance she took. For modern Christians, understanding our identity in Christ is critical. When we recognize that we are God's children, heirs to His promises, and members of His eternal kingdom, the pressures of this world lose their ability to intimidate or sway us.

In today's culture, persecution can take the shape of social isolation, workplace discrimination, or public scorn for holding true to Christian values. Whether it is being labeled intolerant for following biblical morals or experiencing backlash for refusing to participate in unethical workplace practices, Christians today frequently find themselves at variance with social norms. Agnes' experience tells us that standing up for the truth is worthwhile, even if it comes at a high personal cost. She realized that her brief anguish was little compared to the eternal joy that awaited her in heaven.

Agnes' endurance is also seen in her acceptance of suffering as a sort of spiritual victory rather than failure. In today's world, we are frequently taught to avoid suffering or hardship at any cost. However, the Christian religion teaches that tribulations and persecution are a necessary part of the path. Jesus Himself stated, "In this life, you will face difficulties. But do not lose heart! "I overcame the world" (John 16:33). Agnes grasped this reality thoroughly. She confronted her persecutors not with fear or wrath but with the assurance that Christ had already triumphed and that no earthly power could take away the eternal life promised to her.

Similarly, when Christians today suffer trials—whether it be sickness, grief, betrayal, or social exclusion—it is critical to perceive them as chances to grow closer to God. Our sorrow allows us to share in Christ's sufferings, grow in endurance, and refine our faith. Agnes' life demonstrates that suffering is not the conclusion of the story; rather, it is a refinement process that strengthens our link with God and prepares us for the glory that is to come.

Another key feature of Agnes' tenacity is her refusal to let fear control her activities. Fear is a natural human response to danger, but it may also be used by the enemy to paralyze Christians, preventing them from fulfilling God's plan for their lives. Agnes, even at the youthful age of 12 or 13, would not allow fear to govern her. She knew her life was in God's hands, and whatever happened, He would be with her. This strong faith in God's sovereignty enabled her to face her persecutors with a peace beyond comprehension.

Modern Christians frequently experience dread in the form of worry—worry about finances, relationships, professional stability, or the future. But, as Agnes' story reminds us, fear has no place in a heart that completely trusts in God. When we are grounded in faith, terror loses its power over us. Instead of being governed by fear, we are urged to live in the freedom and peace that come from knowing that God is in control of every situation and that He is with us through all of our challenges.

Furthermore, Agnes' courage in the face of persecution serves as a model for how Christians today can respond to opposition. She did not strike out or seek vengeance on those who attempted to harm her. Instead, she maintained a peaceful dignity and peace, knowing that God would be her protector. In today's polarized and hostile environment, it can be tempting to respond to persecution or criticism with violence or defensiveness. However, Agnes demonstrates that true power rests in meekness and humility, in trusting that God would vindicate us in His time.

Christians today must respond to personal attacks or societal criticism with love, compassion, and unshakeable faith. Rather than participating in pointless debates or letting bitterness grow, we are asked to follow Agnes' example by being firm in our convictions while reflecting Christ's compassion and peace.

In practical terms, how can modern Christians nurture such fortitude in the face of persecution? First and foremost, we must prioritize our connection with Christ over anything else. To lay a solid foundation of faith, we must, like Agnes, root our identity in Him by spending time in prayer, scripture, and worship. When our faith is deeply founded, difficulties will not shake us because we are anchored in the truth of who God is and who we are through Him.

Second, we must surround ourselves with a faith community that will support and encourage us during difficult times. Agnes was part of a wider Christian community in Rome, and although many were tormented, they found strength in one another. Similarly, modern Christians require the support of the church—a community of faith that prays together, supports one another, and stands unified in the face of adversity.

Finally, we must remember that our ultimate reward is not worldly approval but Christ's eternal glory. Just as Agnes looked beyond her immediate sorrow to the eternal joy of being united with her Savior, we must also focus on the promises of heaven. The difficulties we endure in this life are transient, but the joy that awaits us in eternity is eternal.

Finally, Agnes' narrative is more than just a martyrdom story; it demonstrates the strength of faith, tenacity, and steadfast dedication to Christ. Her life is an encouragement to all Christians, telling us that even in the midst of persecution, we may remain steady, knowing that we are never alone and that our faith will see us through any adversity. Her example inspires us to persist, knowing that God's grace is adequate and that His strength is made perfect in our weakness.

MIRACLES OF DEFIANCE: Protected By God's Grace

Agnes and the Fire

In the midst of her trial, while Agnes stood firm before the Roman authorities, a powerful and miraculous demonstration of divine protection occurred. The scene was set, with Agnes surrounded by a jeering audience, ready to face the consequences of her steadfast faith. The governor's orders were clear: if she refused to recant her Christian views, she would be exposed to a harrowing ordeal designed to drive her to submit. And yet, what happened next was nothing short of a divine intervention, a powerful demonstration of God's protective grace.

The Roman authorities, anxious to break Agnes' spirit, ordered that she be thrown into a flaming furnace—a manner of punishment designed not only to kill but also to humiliate and frighten. The furnace was filled with raging flames, a brutal reminder of the empire's strength and the awful fate that awaited those who disobeyed it. The audience watched with a mix of excitement and terror, ready to see the outcome of this dramatic clash between pagan authority and firm faith.

As Agnes was led to the furnace, the air was dense with tension. The flames leapt high, their heat radiating outward, a stark reminder of the brutality that awaited her. Onlookers, including Roman residents and inquisitive passersby, held their breath as they waited for the small girl to be devoured by the fire. This was going to be the ultimate test of her faith—a literal trial by fire.

Yet, in a show that defied all natural explanation, something extraordinary happened. As Agnes was led to the opening of the furnace, a profound silence fell over the scene. The flames, which had been ferocious and untamed moments before, appeared to pause, as if waiting for a command. The crowd gasped as they observed an incredible sight: the flames began to move in a purposeful pattern, building an arch that appeared to protect Agnes from the heat.

The soldiers, perplexed and unsure of what they were seeing, hesitated. The governor, sitting on his elevated platform, watched in bewilderment. It was as though the fire itself had been commanded to refrain from touching the innocent girl who stood before it. Agnes, meanwhile, remained composed, her faith unshaken. She did not flinch or cry out; instead, she stared calmly at the flames, her eyes filled with a serene confidence that reflected her unwavering faith in God.

To the astonishment of everyone present, the fire did not consume Agnes. Instead, it danced around her like a protective barrier. The intense heat that should have scorched her had miraculously disappeared. Agnes stood undisturbed, untouched by the flames; her hair and garments were not singed, and her skin was not even scorched. The miraculous protection was so clear and so extraordinary that even those who had come to witness her death were left speechless.

In that moment, God's miraculous intervention was undeniable. It was a tremendous symbol of heavenly protection, demonstrating that God's grace remained with Agnes even in the face of the most horrific threats. The flames, which were supposed to be instruments of death, became symbols of God's power and presence. The miracle of the fire was not only a witness to Agnes' faith but also a powerful reminder of God's supremacy over all earthly forces.

The sight of Agnes standing unharmed before the furnace had a profound impact on everyone there. The crowd, which had initially cheered for her death, was now filled with awe and fear. Many people began to question the legitimacy of the pagan gods they had worshiped, wondering if the Christian God was the actual power. Some were moved to tears, others were filled with a sense of dread, and still others began to whisper among themselves about the miraculous nature of what they had witnessed.

Governor Aspasius, though visibly shaken, attempted to regain control of the situation. He ordered the flames to be intensified, hoping that a more fierce fire might finally force Agnes into submission. Yet, even as the heat grew more intense, the protective barrier persisted. The flames blazed, rising higher and higher, yet they did not reach Agnes. It seemed as if a divine shield encircled her, protecting her from the blazing fire.

The show grabbed the attention of many in the city, and word of the amazing incident traveled swiftly. People from all walks of life gathered to witness the wonder, and soon Agnes' narrative began to catch the attention of many who had previously been indifferent or antagonistic to Christianity. Her miraculous preservation in the furnace became a powerful testament to the Christian faith, a living proof of the God who intervenes on behalf of His people.

The fire miracle was not only a dramatic display of divine protection, but it also provided powerful confirmation of Agnes' faith. It emphasized the idea that God's grace can overcome even the most formidable challenges and that His power is not limited by human understanding or the physical realm. For

Agnes, the miraculous protection was a testament to her faithfulness and a sign that her faith in God was justified.

As Agnes was finally removed from the vicinity of the furnace, unharmed and radiant, the governor and his officials were left grappling with the implications of what they had just witnessed. They could not ignore the clear message: Agnes' God was real, and His power was undeniable. Despite their best efforts to break her spirit, they only succeeded in magnifying her faith's miraculous nature.

Reflecting on Agnes' experience can inspire and encourage modern Christians. The account of her miraculous protection serves as a striking reminder that God is with us in our hardships, even when we cannot see or feel His presence. It teaches us that, no matter how dire the circumstances, God's grace can provide protection, comfort, and strength beyond our understanding. Agnes' unwavering faith and the divine intervention she witnessed inspire us to believe in God's promises and persevere in our own faith journeys.

As we face the metaphorical fires in our own lives—whether they are health challenges, financial difficulties, or personal conflicts—we can take comfort in knowing that God's protection is always available. Just as Agnes was protected by divine favor, we can rely on God to see us through our trials, knowing that His might is greater than any obstacle we may face.

The Conversion of Witnesses

The remarkable events surrounding Agnes' trial had a profound and far-reaching impact on those who observed them. Her steadfast faith and the divine intervention she experienced in the furnace not only captivated the spectators but also led to a dramatic shift in their beliefs and convictions. The effect of her trials extended beyond her immediate surroundings, sparking a wave of conversions among those who had initially come to mock or condemn her.

A silent yet powerful transformation was taking place among the crowd in the Roman arena, where the flames danced around Agnes in a miraculous display of divine protection. The onlookers, who had assembled to witness what they believed would be a sad spectacle of religious servitude, were instead presented with an astounding monument to the power of the Christian God. The sight of Agnes, uninjured and glowing amidst the raging flames, was nothing short of awe-inspiring.

As the first shock of the occurrence began to diminish, whispers of wonder and incredulity swept across the throng. Many who had come with hardened hearts due to skepticism or anger were suddenly dealing with intense feelings of awe and terror. The miracle of Agnes' survival in the face of such overwhelming peril was clear, and it sparked something deep inside those who witnessed it.

Onlookers included Roman citizens, soldiers, and official individuals who were either directly involved in the administration of justice or simply spectators of the public spectacle. These folks, who had presumably been conditioned by years of pagan beliefs and rituals, were now presented with a reality that questioned their understanding of the divine. Agnes' miraculous preservation in the furnace was a direct challenge to the pagan gods they had long worshipped, and it opened their eyes to the possibility of a higher, more powerful deity.

One of the first groups to be affected were the troops and guards assigned to oversee the execution. These men, used to dealing with criminals and dissenters, were extremely concerned by what they had seen. The sight of Agnes standing unharmed by the fire upended their customary processes and expectations. The soldiers, who had become hardened by their duty in carrying out the Roman Empire's orders, were confronted with an instance of divine intervention that they could not comprehend. Their beliefs and pagan rituals were questioned by many. This questioning led to a genuine curiosity about the Christian faith, which, in many cases, turned into a conversion experience.

Similarly, the Roman officials, who were accustomed to exercising authority and enforcing laws with little regard for the individuals subjected to their decisions, found themselves grappling with the implications of Agnes' miraculous survival. The governor and his aides, despite their attempts to maintain control over the situation, were unable to ignore the undeniable evidence of divine intervention. The sight of Agnes, uninjured and tranquil, had a tremendous effect on their worldview. Some of these officials, who had been helpful in carrying out the instructions against Christians, began to face severe internal turmoil. The understanding that their deeds had been challenged by a higher force led to a reevaluation of their own beliefs and behaviors.

The general public was also affected by Agnes' trial. The gathering, which initially came to witness what they assumed would be a demonstration of Christian defeat, found themselves in amazement of the young girl's persistent faith and the remarkable protection she got. As news of the miracle spread, it became a topic of discussion throughout Rome. The story of Agnes, the girl who survived the flames unscathed, became a striking testimony to the Christian faith. People who had previously been indifferent or hostile to Christianity began to question their own beliefs. The miracle not only confirmed the reality of Agnes' faith but also served as a spur for many to study Christianity for themselves.

In the days following the event, Agnes' trial's ripple effects continued to spread. Converts were made not merely among those who had witnessed the miracle directly but also among those who learned about it through word of mouth or hearsay. These witnesses' conversion was not a simple or superficial shift. It involves a profound transformation of heart and intellect, propelled by the undeniable proof of God's power and the powerful witness of Agnes' faith.

For many, conversion was accompanied by a strong and sincere commitment to the Christian faith. The miraculous nature of Agnes' protection as well as the subsequent changes in their own lives inspired these new believers to embrace Christianity with zeal and dedication, often accompanied by a willingness to face their own trials and persecutions. Agnes' tale became a strong symbol of faith and perseverance, urging others to follow her lead and commit to the road of Christian discipleship.

The conversions of the witnesses at Agnes' trial had a far-reaching impact on early Christian society. As more people from various backgrounds and positions of authority came to accept Christianity, the faith began to gain traction in Roman society. The miraculous events surrounding Agnes demonstrated the power of the Christian God while also challenging the mainstream pagan beliefs of the day. This shift in perspective was critical to the eventual spread and foundation of Christianity in the Roman Empire.

Reflecting on the conversion of Agnes' witnesses, modern Christians can be inspired and encouraged by the transformative power of divine intervention. Just as Agnes' steadfastness and the miracle of her protection caused a profound change in the hearts of those who witnessed it, our own acts of faith and testimony can have a similar impact on those around us. By living out our religion with integrity and courage, we have the capacity to touch others in ways that we may not always see or comprehend.

The story of Agnes and the conversion of her witnesses reminds us that God's power is at work in the world and that even in the most challenging situations, His grace can bring about profound and enduring change. As we confront our own hardships and witness to our faith, we can take solace in knowing that our perseverance can have a profound impact on others around us, causing them to experience the transformative power of God's compassion and grace.

The Power of Witness: Martyrdom as a Catalyst

Saint Agnes' story, marked by her suffering and miraculous protection, is a powerful testimony to martyrdom's transformative effect on the spread of the Christian faith. Her persistent dedication and the divine intervention she witnessed not only cemented her status as a respected person in Christian history but also acted as a catalyst for the conversion of countless more. Far from being a mere event of personal pain, Agnes' martyrdom became a powerful beacon of faith, inspiring and attracting countless people to Christianity.

Martyrdom in the early Christian culture was more than just enduring physical pain; it was viewed as a strong message to the faith. The term "martyr" is derived from the Greek word for "witness." For early Christians, the fortitude and steadfastness of martyrs such as Agnes served as ultimate evidence to the truth of their beliefs. Agnes' suffering was more than just a test of personal endurance; it was a public demonstration of faith that struck a profound chord with all who saw or heard about it.

The miraculous circumstances surrounding Agnes' trial greatly contributed to her martyrdom's significance. The miraculous protection she received in front of the flaming furnace was a startling demonstration of God's power and presence. This miracle, observed by many, proved the Christian God's superiority over Rome's pagan deities. For those who were initially suspicious or antagonistic to Christianity, Agnes' miraculous preservation served as a persuasive argument for the truth of her faith.

Agnes' narrative was immediately transmitted throughout Rome and abroad, carried by the tongues of those who had experienced the miracle personally. Her narrative rippled across the city's streets, in marketplaces, and among the intellectual and religious communities of the day. The narrative of a young girl who braved the full fury of the Roman Empire's punishing machinery and survived unhurt thanks to divine protection became a captivating and persuasive account. Many people were moved by this narrative of faith, fortitude, and miraculous deliverance.

The narrative of Agnes spread to people from all walks of life, including Romans, visitors, pagans, and potential converts. Her martyrdom underscored the stark contrast between the ephemeral power of worldly rulers and the eternal sovereignty of the Christian God. This difference was especially striking in a society accustomed to Roman rule, making Agnes' heavenly protection a powerful testimonial to the Christian faith.

Agnes' martyrdom had an equally enormous influence on the Christian community. Her narrative has become a strong emblem of faith's strength and purity. For early Christians, Agnes' narrative was more than just a chronicle of one person's suffering; it was also a source of inspiration and encouragement. It reaffirmed their notion that unwavering faith might win over the most terrible adversities. Her narrative became a rallying point for believers, urging them to uphold their religion with the same courage and conviction that Agnes had exhibited.

The impact of Agnes' martyrdom went beyond the instant conversion of individuals. It contributed to a more general shift in cultural attitudes toward Christianity. The early Christian church was not only growing in size, but it was also gaining respect and influence within the Roman Empire. The legends of martyrs such as Agnes contributed to challenging and finally undermining paganism's power. Her suffering and the miraculous nature of her trials made a strong case for Christianity, demonstrating its persistence and divine protection in the face of persecution.

Agnes' martyrdom also influenced the formation of Christian rites and traditions around martyrdom and sainthood. Her narrative inspired Christians to understand and honor those who suffered for their beliefs. The adoration of martyrs, such as Agnes, influenced Christian liturgical customs, as well as the development of hagiography, or the chronicling of saints' biographies. Her example set the standard for the Christian tradition of honoring martyrs and deriving inspiration from their efforts.

Agnes' story is still relevant to current beliefs. Her pain and the amazing protection she received demonstrate that faith can be a powerful force for change. Her story challenges current Christians to reflect on the depth of their devotion and how their own spiritual experiences can serve as witnesses to others. The narrative of Agnes urges believers to consider how their actions and faith affect those around them, pushing others to seek out and embrace Christianity's transformational power.

Agnes' sacrifice exemplifies the power of witness, demonstrating that faith can serve as a light of hope and transformation even in the midst of adversity. It reminds us that acts of courage and steadfastness in our own lives can have a profound impact on others, inspiring them to seek and embrace the faith.

Agnes' tale impressed many people at the time, and it continues to inspire believers now, emphasizing the enduring power of faith and extraordinary ways in which God can work through His followers' afflictions.

God's Grace in Modern Life

Reflecting on Saint Agnes' tale and the supernatural protection she received, it is apparent that her example has immense value for Christians today. Her unwavering faith and the divine favor she received serve as a timeless reminder of God's ongoing presence and protection in the lives of believers. As we face the complexities and hardships of modern life, Agnes' tale reminds us to reflect on how God's grace manifests itself in our own spiritual journey.

In comparison to the dramatic miracles of the past, the concept of supernatural protection and direction today may appear vague. However, the essence of God's grace is just as vital today as it was in Agnes' time. God's protection and direction in modern life may take other forms, but they are no less important. Believers frequently discover that God's mercy works through small, everyday miracles and deep times of reassurance, strengthening their confidence and sustaining them through adversity.

One of the most captivating features of Agnes' story is her steadfast determination in the face of persecution. Her life displays a profound trust in God's providence, which allowed her to bear extreme strain and danger. This story serves as a wonderful model for modern Christians as they face their own issues. Just as Agnes relied on God's grace to get through her sufferings, believers today are required to rely on God's protection and guidance, even when the way ahead appears uncertain or tough.

In modern times, God's protection is frequently manifested through many types of support and sustenance. Individuals may receive unexpected respite during times of financial stress, comfort during times of grief, or strength when dealing with personal difficulties. These instances, while not involving miraculous interventions as those experienced during Agnes' time, are still symbols of God's grace. They serve as reminders that God's presence and concern are palpable, even in the face of daily problems.

Furthermore, the community of faith is essential in reflecting God's grace. Just as Agnes' narrative inspired and strengthened the early Christian community, the sympathy and solidarity of fellow believers today can be extremely encouraging. Churches, faith groups, and Christian organizations frequently provide practical support, spiritual direction, and a sense of connection. This collective support is an expression of God's grace, illustrating how His love and protection are communicated through the actions of others.

Personal spiritual experiences in modern life reflect God's constant direction. Many Christians can recall times when they felt a strong sense of direction or clarity in their lives, especially during times of prayer or reflection. These heavenly guiding experiences may manifest as inner promptings, insightful counsel from others, or calm settlement of difficult situations. Such times demonstrate that God remains actively involved in the lives of His people, guiding them with the same care and attention that Agnes received.

Furthermore, the narrative of Agnes emphasizes the significance of perseverance in religion. Her unrelenting dedication, even in the face of adversity, inspires modern Christians to acquire a similar tenacity. In a society full of diversions and challenges to faith, adhering to spiritual beliefs and practices can provide strength and peace. Agnes' example tells believers that persevering in faith in the face of adversity is a way to experience and witness God's grace.

It is also worth mentioning that the current setting brings a distinct set of obstacles and opportunities for encountering God's grace. Social injustice, personal hardships, and global catastrophes can all put a person's faith to the test. However, within these hardships, there are frequently stories of compassion, hope, and transformation that recall the heavenly protection and guidance experienced in Agnes' time. Whether via acts of generosity, personal growth, or overcoming adversity, God's grace remains visible in the lives of those who remain faithful.

When considering God's grace in modern life, it is crucial to remember that supernatural protection and guidance do not always include miraculous happenings. They also discuss the daily, often unnoticed ways in which God helps and strengthens His people. This concept allows believers to comprehend the continuity of God's care from ancient times to the present. Agnes' tale connects the past and the present, reminding us that God's grace is a living, active force that shapes and sustains our lives even now.

Finally, Saint Agnes' tale inspires us to be steady in our faith, to believe in God's protection and guidance, and to recognize His grace in both remarkable and regular circumstances. In doing so, we respect the history of saints like Agnes while also affirming the continued relevance of God's mercy in our own spiritual journeys. As we face our own hardships and endeavor to live out our faith, we can be inspired by Agnes' example, knowing that God's grace is with us, guiding and protecting us just as it was with her.

THE FINAL STAND: A Crown Of Martyrdom

The Execution Order

As the time came for Agnes to face the ultimate decree, the city of Rome was filled with tangible suspense and fear. The once-bustling streets appeared hushed, the typical clatter of daily life muffled in the shadow of the coming execution. It was time for Agnes, the young Christian martyr whose unwavering faith had perplexed the authorities, to undergo the last test of her devotion. This was a dramatic and tense moment in which a young girl's willpower contrasted sharply with the Roman Empire's iron will.

The order for Agnes' execution was given with solemnity, reflecting the seriousness with which the Roman authorities treated the situation. The edict, given with cold efficiency, marked the end of a series of events in which Agnes had been tested at every turn. The Roman governor, motivated by a desire to establish his dominance and dampen Christianity's rising influence, decided that it was time to make an example of her. This was more than just a choice to carry out a punishment; it was an act aimed to reestablish the official religion's primacy while suppressing the swelling tide of Christian faith.

In the execution room, the atmosphere was one of grim determination and underlying tension. Despite their experience dealing with the condemned, the officials and soldiers were startled by the sharp contrast between the gravity of the situation and the calm manner of the young girl in front of them. Agnes, who was only a teenager, maintained a calm and steady resolve that appeared to defy the gravity of the situation. Her faith, honed in the crucible of her previous experiences, now shone with clarity, making her a beacon of courage in the face of fear.

The death order was given with the emotionless efficiency expected of Roman bureaucracy. It was a decree that showed little concern for personal feelings, a glaring reminder of the cold, administrative nature of the Empire's court system. The order called for Agnes' execution in public, with the intention of making her death a forceful statement against the expanding Christian movement. The decision was definitive, and the machinery of Roman justice was put into action with an unsettling sense of inevitability.

However, the seriousness of the situation did not appear to weigh on Agnes. Despite the impending execution, she remained calm and courageous. Her demeanor demonstrated the strength of her faith, which had already been tried and proven through public scorn, suffering, and miraculous survival. Her fearlessness sprang not from naivety or irresponsibility but from a genuine sense that her life and death were in the hands of a higher power.

As the time approached, individuals on the scene could not help but notice the stark contrast between the young girl and the surrounding officials. The troops, despite carrying out their jobs with the required professionalism, were noticeably impacted by Agnes' serenity. They were trained to perform their jobs with detachment, but the seriousness of the situation, mixed with the calm courage of the condemned, created an atmosphere fraught with unspoken tension. The stark contrast between the military efficiency of the execution preparations and Agnes' calm acceptance showed the fundamental gap between worldly power and spiritual conviction.

Agnes' faith was now more than just a personal witness; it was a public declaration. Her determination to face execution without abandoning her ideas was a stunning statement that screamed more than words ever could. It was a defiant stance against the Empire's desire to obliterate the Christian faith, and it would reverberate well beyond the immediate vicinity of the execution site.

The audience that assembled to see the execution consisted of interested passersby, doubting pagans, and devout Christians. For some, this was an opportunity to witness the death of a contentious person; for others, it was a time for solemn meditation and prayer. The audience's variety highlighted the importance of Agnes' dying moments—not only as a personal trial but as a momentous event with ramifications for the entire community. Her execution was more than a show; it was a moment that would be remembered and recounted, shaping people's attitudes about Christianity.

Agnes was escorted to the execution site, and the air was thick with expectancy. The solemn march through the streets was characterized by almost respectful silence, in stark contrast to Rome's customary noise and activity. The public execution was intended to be a spectacle, a chilling warning of the consequences of resisting the Empire's authority. However, Agnes' persistence and unwavering presence transformed this moment of intimidation into one of deep importance.

Agnes' demeanor remained unchanged in the final seconds before her execution. She approached her death with a calmness that appeared to transcend the circumstances, her faith protecting her from the dread of the coming doom. Her fearlessness in the face of such tremendous adversity was a remarkable demonstration of the strength of her conviction, which had been tested and confirmed through numerous trials.

The execution order was more than just a directive; it was a pivotal moment in history and spirituality. Agnes' worldly journey came to an end, and her legacy as a martyr began. Her daring acceptance of death and unflinching faith in the face of execution would serve as a source of inspiration for future generations, demonstrating the enduring power of divine grace and human conviction.

Agnes' Last Prayer

In the tense environment of her closing moments, Agnes' final prayer stands out as a moving witness to her persistent faith and strong spiritual conviction. This final act, performed on the verge of execution, shows a moment of peaceful yet profound intensity, demonstrating her unwavering determination to meet Christ.

As Agnes was escorted to the execution site, the gravity of the situation became palpable. The circumstances, packed with solemnity and suspense, provided a striking background for her final prayer. The atmosphere was dense with the crowd's hushed murmuring and the Roman soldiers' stiff, stoic posture. Despite this stress, Agnes remained a figure of outstanding calm and grace.

Agnes' farewell prayer is regarded as reverent and profoundly spiritual. She is claimed to have raised her eyes to heaven, her look filled with a peaceful conviction that testified of her strong faith and unwavering connection to the almighty. In this hallowed moment, her words were more than just a plea; they were a confession of her unwavering belief and an affirmation of her willingness to completely embrace her faith, even in the face of death.

Her prayer demonstrated her spiritual preparation and entire trust in God. Agnes is said to have prayed not for salvation from her fate but for the courage to face it with dignity and grace. Her words demonstrated an enduring dedication to her faith and a sincere wish to be with Christ in the afterlife. This prayer was more than just a personal expression; it was a profound statement about her spiritual path and connection with God.

The content of Agnes' prayer is frequently described in terms of simplicity and depth. She reportedly spoke of her faith in Christ, stating her desire to be united with Him in eternal life. Her statements were infused with peace and assurance, demonstrating her deep faith in God's plan and her acceptance of her coming martyrdom as part of a divine purpose. This final prayer summed up her entire life's commitment to Christ and marked the end of her spiritual journey.

In the face of impending death, Agnes' prayer emphasized her deep forgiveness and love. She is supposed to have pleaded with God for mercy not only for herself but also for those who would carry out her execution. This act of forgiveness exemplified her Christian ideals and demonstrated her awareness of the divine essence of love and grace. Her ability to forgive in such a difficult personal situation demonstrates her spiritual maturity and connection with Christ's teachings.

Agnes' dying moments, accented by her prayer, were filled with a genuine sense of serenity. Her calm acceptance of her fate and emphasis on her spiritual beliefs provided a dramatic contrast to the terrible reality of her execution. This calm manner, along with her deep faith, left an indelible impression on those who watched her last moments. The prayer became a testament to faith's ability to transcend earthly anxieties and sufferings, providing a glimpse into Agnes' transcendent tranquility.

The significance of Agnes' final prayer extends beyond her immediate martyrdom. It is a striking emblem of the transformational power of faith and the ultimate tranquility that comes from living in accordance with divine principles. Agnes' final prayer teaches modern readers and believers a powerful message about faith and acceptance. It encourages others to reflect on how they might approach their own hardships and challenges with the same calm and resolve that Agnes exhibited.

Agnes' prayer has ongoing resonance in the Christian tradition. It emphasizes the significance of spiritual readiness and the effectiveness of prayer as a means of communicating with God. Her final words serve as a reminder of faith's ultimate goal: to unite with Christ and live a life characterized by divine love and grace. The serenity of her final moments serves as a powerful model for believers to approach their own spiritual journeys, regardless of the difficulties they may face.

To summarize, Agnes' final prayer is a powerful expression of her faith and eagerness to meet Christ. It captures the essence of her spiritual journey and serves as a powerful testament to the strength and peace that come from a strong and unwavering faith. Her prayer, which is characterized by peace, forgiveness, and a firm commitment to her beliefs, continues to inspire and guide believers, reminding them of the ultimate goal of faith and the transformative power of Divine Grace.

Martyrdom as Victory

The concept of martyrdom is deeply rooted in Christian theology, and it is frequently viewed as a form of ultimate victory rather than mere suffering or defeat. Agnes' death, rather than being a source of despair, represents a triumphant entry into eternal life with Christ. This perspective on martyrdom emphasizes the transformative nature of faith as well as the profound value of witnessing to one's faith even in death.

In Christian theology, martyrdom is inextricably linked to the concept of victory by sacrifice. The term "martyr" is derived from the Greek word "martys," which means "witness." A martyr is someone who bears witness to their faith, often at the cost of their life. This ultimate act of witness is regarded as a significant testimony to the strength and reality of the Christian faith. Martyrdom, for early Christians like Agnes, was viewed as a sacred and victorious climax of their spiritual path, rather than a sorrowful ending.

Agnes' death was viewed as a win since it revealed her unwavering devotion to Christ. By choosing to face execution rather than renounce her faith, Agnes exemplified the ultimate expression of love and dedication. This act of defiance against the pagan authorities was seen not as a defeat but as a triumphant declaration of her belief in the promise of eternal life with Christ. Her willingness to endure suffering for the sake of her faith highlighted the deep conviction that her earthly life was but a prelude to a far greater spiritual reality.

The theology of martyrdom emphasizes that true victory is attained through the steadfast enduring of suffering and persecution. This attitude is anchored in the teachings of Jesus Christ, who Himself endured pain and death as a means of guaranteeing the salvation of humanity. In the New Testament, Christ's suffering and crucifixion are viewed as the ultimate victory over sin and death. By following in Christ's footsteps, martyrs like Agnes are thought to partake in this victory, their deaths serving as a strong message to the continuing truth of the Gospel.

Agnes' martyrdom might be interpreted as a fulfillment of her worldly mission and a celebration of her final union with Christ. In Christian doctrine, martyrdom is typically related to the idea of a "crown of righteousness" granted to individuals who suffer for their faith. This concept is represented in the works of early Christian Fathers and in the biblical passages that speak of the rewards awaiting those who remain faithful unto death. Agnes' death was thus not just a sorrowful tragedy but also a wonderful occasion in which she was exalted to a position of dignity in the celestial kingdom.

Martyrdom's victory is also shown in its impact on the larger Christian community. The story of Agnes, her courage, and her ultimate sacrifice is a powerful source of inspiration and encouragement for Christians. Her martyrdom emphasized the early Christian message, demonstrating that faith in Christ could resist even the most severe afflictions. This creates a ripple effect on the faith community, increasing the determination of other believers and reinforcing the truth of Christian beliefs.

Furthermore, the concept of martyrdom as victory is deeply embedded in the Christian understanding of suffering and redemption. In this view, suffering is not seen as a meaningless or futile experience but as a transformative process that brings believers closer to God. Martyrs' sufferings are thought to be redemptive, contributing to spiritual progress in both individuals and communities. In this setting, Agnes' death served as a strong testimonial to the redeeming nature of suffering, revealing that faith and hope may triumph even in the face of death.

The theology of martyrdom emphasizes the concept of solidarity with Christ. Martyrs, by enduring suffering and death for their faith, are thought to get into profound oneness with Christ's. This solidarity is viewed as a sort of spiritual contact that extends beyond earthly existence, leading to a better experience of divine love and grace. Agnes' martyrdom thus represents not only a personal victory but also a profound expression of her unity with Christ's own suffering and triumph.

In reflecting on Agnes' martyrdom as a victory, it is essential to understand that this victory is not confined to the individual but extends to the broader Christian community. The lives and sacrifices of martyrs like Agnes contribute to the continuous story of the Church, providing a monument to the enduring power of faith. Their experiences inspire and push people to live out their faith with the same courage and conviction, reinforcing the concept that true success is found in faithfully witnessing one's life and actions.

Finally, Agnes' martyrdom exemplifies the deeply held Christian notion that true victory comes through loyalty and sacrifice. Her death was a triumphant confession of her faith in Christ and the culmination of her spiritual journey. By accepting martyrdom, Agnes not only validated her own faith but also became a light of encouragement for the Christian community. Her tale serves as a striking reminder of the transformative power of faith and the enduring promise of eternal life with Christ, reinforcing that martyrdom, far from being a failure, is the ultimate victory in the Christian faith.

Martyrs Today: The Call to Courage

Agnes' legacy as a valiant martyr extends far beyond her historical context, resonates powerfully with the experiences of current martyrs. Her tale is a remarkable illustration of how profound faith and commitment to truth can transcend time and space, offering as a source of inspiration for those facing persecution today. Agnes' call to courage is reflected in many people's lives today, pushing us to consider our own dedication to truth and faith, even when it comes at a considerable personal cost.

Modern-day martyrs, while not necessarily in the spotlight, continue to undergo hardships and persecution for their commitment to their convictions. Their stories are diverse, spanning nations, religions, and circumstances, but they have one common thread with Agnes: an unflinching commitment to their convictions in the face of agony or death. These people, like Agnes, face daunting obstacles with fortitude that defies worldly worries, demonstrating the ageless character of the call to faithfulness and the powerful impact of leading a life dedicated to truth.

One important component of Agnes' story that resonates with modern martyrs is the concept of remaining firm in the face of opposition. Despite the enormous pressures and threats she experienced, Agnes refused to forsake her Christian faith, which reflects the experiences of contemporary believers facing persecution. Modern martyrs reflect Agnes' resilience and determination, whether in places where religious freedoms are restricted or in circumstances where standing out for one's beliefs can result in serious consequences. Their boldness exemplifies the idea that true devotion to one's ideals frequently necessitates defying existing standards and social forces.

The current call to courage includes not only confronting bodily threats but also navigating subtle kinds of persecution and challenge. In many parts of the world, believers may experience social exclusion, economic hardship, or personal and professional consequences for their faith. These challenges, while not in the same form as Agnes' physical suffering, are substantial and necessitate a similar level of determination. The bravery to keep one's principles in the face of such adversity displays Agnes' spiritual strength and integrity.

Furthermore, modern-day martyrs demonstrate the broader ramifications of living a life of commitment. These people's courage is a stunning testament to faith's transformational power. Their experiences encourage others to think about their own ideals and ponder how they may stand up for truth in their own lives. This thought frequently leads to a more in-depth knowledge of the sacrifices required to honestly live out one's faith, as well as a renewed desire to uphold one's principles with integrity and courage.

Agnes' story also serves as a reminder about the larger spiritual framework in which modern martyrs function. The experiences of contemporary believers suffering persecution frequently depend on the same spiritual foundations that led Agnes. This shared faith supports the idea that the struggles of today's martyrs are part of a bigger story of faithfulness and divine purpose. Looking to the example of Agnes and other saints can provide present believers with comfort and solace, knowing that their trials are part of a centuries-long continuity of testimony.

In addition to personal courage, the story of Agnes and modern martyrs emphasizes the value of community support and solidarity. Just as Agnes' courage inspired and strengthened the early Christian community, the sufferings of modern martyrs frequently elicit sympathy and advocacy from their faith groups and beyond. This collective response not only gives physical assistance, but it also promotes a sense of shared mission and purpose, supporting the concept that standing up for truth is a group effort that transcends individual obstacles.

The call to courage includes a commitment to creating settings in which religion and truth might flourish. This could involve fighting for religious freedom, assisting groups that defend persecuted believers, and participating in discussions that foster understanding and respect among different faith traditions. By addressing the root causes of persecution and striving to make the world a more just and compassionate place, believers can remember the legacy of martyrs like Agnes while also contributing to a global atmosphere that fosters courage and conviction.

Finally, Agnes' narrative invites us to reflect on our own lives and how we might respond to the call to courage in our respective settings. Her unwavering faith, even in the face of death, is a striking reminder of the strength and grace that come from living a truth-centered life. In reflecting on her legacy, current believers are encouraged to embrace the call to be steadfast in their convictions, to assist and inspire those who experience persecution, and to live out their faith with the same courage and integrity that Agnes demonstrated.

In conclusion, Agnes' narrative of martyrdom and courage continues to inspire and motivate modern believers to stand up for truth, even at tremendous personal cost. Contemporary martyrs' experiences mirror hers, emphasizing the timeless call to devotion and bravery. By drawing on the lessons of Agnes and other saints, believers can find the fortitude to face their own challenges and contribute to a world where truth and conviction are defended with steadfast dedication.

AFTERMATH: The Legacy of St. Agnes

The Immediate Impact of Her Death

The death of St. Agnes was more than just a historical event; it was a momentous moment that echoed throughout Rome and beyond, leaving an indelible mark on the early Christian community and beyond. Following her martyrdom, the city experienced a stunning outpouring of veneration and a significant transformation in its spiritual environment.

In the days following Agnes' execution, the Roman public and early Christians expressed profound awe and sadness. The dramatic nature of her martyrdom, along with her youth and unwavering faith, made a gripping story that captured many people's hearts and minds. Agnes' courage in the face of death became a strong symbol of Christian virtue and resilience, encouraging both immediate and long-term transformation in society.

Agnes' death elicited a complicated reaction from Roman officials and pagan citizens alike. While the execution was intended to prevent others from becoming Christians, it had the opposite effect. Rather than stifling the growth of the new faith, Agnes' sacrifice sparked intense enthusiasm among believers and observers alike. Her tale served as a rallying point for the Christian community, strengthening their resolve and emboldening their testimony in the face of persecution.

One of the most significant immediate consequences of Agnes' martyrdom was the conversion of hearts. The dramatic narrative of her persistent faith and miraculous survival in the face of persecution struck a chord with many. Those who witnessed her trial and death were often struck by her poise and seeming elegance. The outcome was a rush of conversions among both skeptical and anti-Christians.

The Christian community in Rome, despite being a minority and under peril, felt a newfound feeling of optimism and camaraderie. Agnes' martyrdom served as a powerful example of ultimate sacrifice and the tremendous strength that comes from faith. This not only encouraged existing believers but also drew in new followers who were moved by her narrative. The story of Agnes became a source of encouragement and a compelling testimony to the transformative power of the Christian faith.

The adoration bestowed on Agnes reflected the response to her death. Her martyrdom immediately sparked a devotional cult around her memory. Early Christians revered Agnes as a saint, and her narrative was told in sermons, literature, and oral traditions. Her martyrdom was celebrated with a variety of ceremonies and practices, including the creation of a feast day in her honor. This adoration was more than just a ritual; it was a profound statement of the early Christian community's respect and love for her.

Agnes' burial site became a popular pilgrimage and devotional destination. The catacombs of Rome, where Agnes was buried, quickly became a site of veneration and reverence. Pilgrims flocked from all over to visit her tomb, hoping to honor her legacy and be inspired by her example. The place became a symbol of hope and faith, representing the long-term impact of her life and death.

In addition to encouraging conversions and devotion, Agnes' sacrifice had a significant impact on the overall Christian narrative. Her biography was woven into the greater tapestry of early Christian history and theology, acting as a compelling model of Christian virtue and the ultimate testimonial to faith. The narratives of her life and death helped to shape the Christian notion of martyrdom and sainthood, influencing how future generations perceived and appreciated the sacrifices of early Christians.

Agnes' martyrdom had an immediate impact on Rome's larger cultural and social setting. As her narrative spread, it challenged traditional pagan beliefs and traditions, emphasizing the Christian faith's strength and tenacity. The public character of her execution, as well as the reactions of Christians and pagans, demonstrated Christianity's expanding influence in the Roman world. Agnes' death constituted a watershed moment in the larger fight between paganism and Christianity, indicating a dramatic shift toward a more Christianized culture.

To summarize, the immediate aftermath of St. Agnes' martyrdom had a profound and revolutionary impact on both the early Christian community and Roman society as a whole. Her death prompted conversions, strengthened current believers' faith, and cemented her status as a beloved saint. The reverence and devotion that followed her martyrdom demonstrated the profound significance of her sacrifice and the continuing influence of her example. Agnes' narrative became a tremendous tribute to the power of faith and the importance of standing up for one's beliefs, changing the course of Christian history and inspiring future generations.

The Power of Her Relics

In Christian tradition, the power of relics is profoundly based on the concept that tangible artifacts associated with saints have spiritual meaning. St. Agnes' relics became strong emblems of divine grace and supernatural intervention, instilling a profound sense of devotion and reverence among the devout. The adoration of her relics, as well as the developing devotion surrounding her tomb, are powerful examples of how physical remains can serve as focal points for spiritual experiences and collective faith.

St. Agnes' relics became associated with miraculous events almost immediately after her death. Early Christians believed that her martyrdom confirmed her faith while also leaving a visible proof of heavenly presence. As news of her miracles spread, her grave and relics became places of pilgrimage and adoration. The belief in the miraculous power of relics was based more on the spiritual connection they symbolized to the saint and God's favor than on the bodily remains themselves.

One of Agnes' relics' most well-known miracles was the preservation of her body. According to early Christian beliefs, despite terrible conditions and the passage of time, her remains were discovered incorrupt or miraculously preserved. This preservation was interpreted as a symbol of her holiness and divine favor. The incorruptibility of a saint's body was frequently seen as supernatural evidence of their holiness, boosting faith in their intercessory power and the purity of their relics.

The grave of St. Agnes, located in Rome's catacombs, immediately became a popular veneration site. Pilgrims came from all around to visit her tomb, seeking blessings, healing, and spiritual peace. Her tomb's position in the early Christian catacombs added to its hallowed value. The catacombs, which served as burial and shelter for early Christians, were already filled with holiness and mystery. Agnes' tomb became a focal site in the Christian community, representing the convergence of worldly pain and heavenly reward.

Miraculous healings and answered prayers boosted the reputation of Agnes' relics. Accounts of people who received bodily and spiritual healing via St. Agnes' intercession began to spread. These legends frequently included people who came to her tomb in great faith and desperation, only to leave with their illnesses cured or their spiritual burdens removed. Such miracles were interpreted as evidence of Agnes' sanctity and her ongoing active presence in the lives of the devout. They helped strengthen belief in the saint's intercession power and the sanctity of her relics.

The devotion to St. Agnes' remains extended beyond the physical site of her burial. Her relics were also dispersed across Christian towns and churches, where they continued to inspire reverence and miracles. These relics were frequently stored in ornate reliquaries and were significant objects of devotion. The practice of venerating relics included both physical reverence and spiritual thought. Believers would pray before relics, hoping to become closer to the saint's example and feel a stronger connection to God's grace.

The significance of Agnes' relics went beyond the immediate setting of early Christianity. Her relics became emblematic of the larger Christian tradition of honoring saints and their bodies. This practice reinforced the belief in the communion of saints, which holds that the faithful are spiritually connected over time and geography. St. Agnes' relics, like those of other saints, served as tangible connections to the divine and holy lives of those who came before her.

The devotion to Agnes' relics also influenced the development of Christian art and architecture. Her tomb became a pilgrimage destination, and churches dedicated to her became significant places of devotion and creative expression. The visual portrayals of St. Agnes, as well as the magnificent reliquaries that kept her bones, expressed the significance of her martyrdom and the reverence bestowed upon her. These artistic representations not only honored the saint but also helped to communicate the spiritual lessons and values linked to her life and passing.

In the larger framework of Christian history, the veneration of relics such as St. Agnes' demonstrates the significance of physical items in the church's spiritual life. The belief in the power of relics reinforces the notion that the material world can be used to obtain heavenly grace and interact with the sacred. Agnes' relics, as strong symbols of faith and sanctity, continue to inspire and urge believers to seek a closer connection with God through the saints' example.

Finally, the power of St. Agnes' relics, as well as the devotion that gathered around her tomb, demonstrate the immense spiritual value that Christian tradition places on saints' remains. Her relics became emblems of divine grace, miraculous intervention, and spiritual connection, attracting pilgrims and believers who sought blessings and inspiration. Agnes' adoration of relics demonstrates the long-lasting impact of her life and martyrdom, confirming conviction in the transformational power of faith and the sacredness of saints' remains.

Building a Legacy: The Basilica of St. Agnes

St. Agnes' legacy was preserved and commemorated through the construction of cathedrals dedicated to her memory, with the Basilica of St. Agnes serving as a tribute to her long-lasting influence on the Christian religion. The creation of these sacred locations not only commemorated her martyrdom but also functioned as focal areas for adoration, reflection, and collective worship, instilling her memory firmly in the fabric of Christian life and devotion.

The Basilica of St. Agnes, built on her burial location in Rome's Catacombs, is a notable monument to her legacy. Emperor Constantine and his mother, St. Helena, financed the construction of the first church over her burial in the early Christian period, most likely in the fourth century. This early basilica was a significant step toward establishing St. Agnes as a central figure in Christian worship, ensuring that her memory would be preserved for future generations.

The Basilica of St. Agnes' site was carefully chosen for symbolic reasons. The tombs where her remains were placed were already revered by early Christians. These underground burial sites served as places of refuge and devotion during times of persecution. Early Christians honored her sacrifice by erecting a church over her tomb while also connecting her memory to the sacred space of the catacombs, increasing the spiritual value of the place.

The original basilica's architectural style mirrored early Christian values of simplicity and reverence. It had a classic basilica layout, with a central nave surrounded by aisles and an apse at the end to house the altar and St. Agnes' relics. The church was built to accommodate the expanding number of pilgrims and to support the liturgical rites associated with her devotion. Over time, the basilica became a popular place of Christian devotion, attracting people from all over the Roman Empire who wanted to honor St. Agnes and seek her intercession.

The Basilica of St. Agnes has undergone various modifications and reconstructions over the ages, each of which has helped to preserve and expand her legacy. Notably, Pope Honorius I ordered a major reconstruction in the seventh century, including the construction of a new apse and a splendid entrance. This repair was part of a larger attempt to elevate the basilica's position as a significant pilgrimage destination and accommodate the growing number of devotees.

The church underwent the most extensive rebuilding during the 16th and 17th centuries, when it was renovated by prominent architects such as Girolamo Rainaldi and Francesco Borromini. This period saw the transition from Renaissance to Baroque architecture, and the renovations mirrored the changing artistic and theological emphases of the time. The new basilica had lavish embellishments, such as frescoes and sculptures, honoring St. Agnes' life and martyrdom. These artistic pieces not only commemorated her memory but also told a visual story of her life and the supernatural happenings related to her relics.

The Basilica of St. Agnes remained an important focus of devotion and pilgrimage throughout the Middle Ages and into the contemporary day. On January 21st, the church became a focal point for commemoration of her feast day, attracting hundreds of pilgrims who came to pay their respects and find spiritual inspiration. Her feast day was celebrated annually with processions, prayers, and relic veneration, strengthening her status as a revered saint and ensuring that her legacy remained vibrant and current.

The continued devotion to St. Agnes was reflected in the building of other churches and institutions dedicated to her memory. Throughout Europe and the Christian world, countless churches, chapels, and religious communities have been named for her. These institutions played a role in spreading her story and preserving the custom of commemorating her example. The broad adoration of St. Agnes in many locations demonstrated the international appeal of her life and martyrdom, as well as the significance of her legacy to the global Christian community.

In addition to the architectural cathedrals dedicated to St. Agnes, her memory has been preserved by the ongoing promotion of her story and teachings. Devotional writings, hymns, and liturgical texts commemorating her life and martyrdom have contributed to St. Agnes' continued reverence. These works not only allowed us to reflect on her example, but they also helped to pass her tale down to future generations, guaranteeing that her legacy would live on.

The Basilica of St. Agnes, as well as the larger network of churches and organizations devoted to her memory, demonstrate the significant impact her life and death had on the Christian faith. The tale of St. Agnes was kept, honored, and passed down through the generations thanks to these sacred sites. Her legacy lives on in the architectural and spiritual structures that honor her, inspiring and challenging Christians to live with courage, faith, and dedication.

To summarize, the building and preservation of churches dedicated to St. Agnes, particularly the Basilica of St. Agnes, were critical in honoring her legacy and assuring her continuous presence in the Christian tradition. These sacred areas not only memorialized her martyrdom but also served as places of devotion, pilgrimage, and contemplation. Her legacy's continuing significance demonstrates the strength of faith and the long-term influence of those who live and die for their ideals.

Saints and Legacy: What Will We Leave Behind?

In studying St. Agnes' legacy, readers are challenged to consider the important question of what kind of spiritual legacy they will leave. Agnes' narrative is more than just a historical account; it is a stunning illustration of how one person's faith, determination, and courage can impact the future and inspire countless others. Her life inspires us to think about the impact we can have on those who come after us, as well as how our own actions and ideals can contribute to a lasting faith legacy.

St. Agnes' legacy was built on her strong faith, courage in the face of persecution, and capacity to inspire others by example. Her narrative spans time and space, influencing believers centuries after she died. This enduring effect prompts us to consider the nature of our own legacies and how we may design them to have a significant impact.

To leave a legacy like St. Agnes', one must first live a life of faith and integrity. Agnes' unshakable devotion to Christ, despite the enormous challenges and risks she faced, emphasizes the value of living truly and totally by one's beliefs. For modern readers, this entails investigating how strongly faith influences their daily lives and decisions. Are we dedicated to living our values in a way that is consistent with our beliefs? Are we prepared to remain steadfast in our convictions, even when it is difficult?

Another aspect of leaving a significant legacy is the influence you have on others. St. Agnes' tale is notable for her capacity to inspire and convert others via her actions and suffering. Her life reminds us to consider how our own actions affect people around us. Are we utilizing our skills and resources to create a positive impact on our communities? Are we living in a way that inspires others to seek the truth, compassion, and faith?

The value of leaving a spiritual legacy is reflected in our contributions to our communities and the globe. Like St. Agnes, who inspired a generation and beyond, we are expected to make decisions that represent our values and contribute to the greater good. This could include performing acts of service, participating in philanthropic projects, or simply being a source of support and encouragement to others. Our daily encounters and decisions can leave a legacy of compassion, honesty, and faith that will continue to influence people long after we are gone.

Consider the importance of mentorship and advice in creating a lasting legacy. St. Agnes' example provides a model for how we might mentor others, whether in formal roles or in casual interactions. By sharing our experiences, offering support, and mentoring others on their spiritual journeys, we contribute to the creation of a ripple effect that can reach far beyond our local sphere of impact. Reflecting on how we mentor and encourage others around us can reveal ways to leave a legacy that will benefit future generations of believers.

In addition to our own activities, the legacy we leave behind is formed by how we interact with and contribute to the growth of our religious communities. St. Agnes' impact included not just her personal purity but also how her narrative inspired a larger movement among the Christian community. By actively participating in our religion communities, contributing to their mission, and supporting their efforts, we may ensure that our legacy is part of a wider, continuing effort to live out our values and promote our faith.

As we create our own legacies, remember that the impact of our lives is frequently greater than we realize. Small acts of kindness, moments of courage, and unwavering faith may appear tiny in the short term, but they can have a huge impact over time. St. Agnes' legacy blossomed as a result of her devoted testimony, and our own deeds can help to leave a legacy that inspires and guides others.

When pondering about what we will leave behind, it is useful to contemplate our life's ultimate aims. What do we hope others will remember about us? What ideals and concepts do we want connected with our names? By concentrating on these questions, we can better align our daily lives and actions with the legacy we hope to leave.

Finally, creating a spiritual legacy requires a mix of living genuinely, inspiring others through our actions, positively contributing to our communities, and deeply connecting with our faith. St. Agnes' life is a stunning reminder of the impact that one person's faith may have on the world. Reflecting on her example and seeking to embrace similar ideals in our own lives allows us to leave a lasting legacy that will inspire and uplift future generations.

Finally, the legacy of St. Agnes challenges us to consider how our own lives will be remembered and the impact we aspire to have. By living our faith with honesty, inspiring others, giving back to our communities, and mentoring those around us, we create a spiritual legacy that will last beyond our lifetimes. St. Agnes' tale calls us to live with purpose and leave a legacy of faith, love, and courage that will continue to inspire and alter the world.

AGNES' INFLUENCE ACROSS THE AGES

Medieval Devotion to St. Agnes

During the Middle Ages, St. Agnes' worship grew profoundly and influentially, leading to intensified devotion and the formation of significant religious traditions inspired by her life and purity. Her biography, which included themes of fortitude, unshakable faith, and heavenly protection, struck a deep chord with medieval Christians, inspiring the development of monastic institutions and widespread devotion to her exemplary attributes.

The medieval period, which lasted roughly from the fifth to the fifteenth century, was marked by a strengthening of Christian religion and a greater emphasis on saints' lives as models of devotion and virtue. During this period, St. Agnes' life and sacrifice were especially noteworthy, representing the ideal of purity and enduring faith in the face of persecution. Her narrative was hailed as a remarkable example of Christian goodness, inspiring both laypeople and religious authorities.

One of the most remarkable aspects of medieval devotion to St. Agnes was the formation of monastic organizations dedicated to her memory and inspired by her virtues. St. Agnes Order and Sisters of St. Agnes Congregation were the most notable. These religious communities were formed to mirror Agnes' ideas of purity and dedication. They sought to embody her life's teachings in their own spiritual practices and charity endeavors, maintaining her legacy through acts of dedication and service.

The Order of St. Agnes, created in the 12th century, was especially dedicated to propagating the virtues of chastity and piety that St. Agnes embodied. The order founded numerous convents and monastic institutions around Europe, where members dedicated themselves to a life of prayer, contemplation, and service. The order's rule emphasized the need to maintain purity of heart and spirit, which reflected the virtues for which St. Agnes was known. Members of the order were committed to sustaining high standards of personal purity and communal living so that St. Agnes' example could continue to inspire and lead their spiritual activities.

The Congregation of the Sisters of St. Agnes, established later in the 16th century, depended largely on St. Agnes' legacy. This church was founded with a strong emphasis on education and social service. Sisters dedicated themselves to teaching, nursing, and many forms of social work, hoping to bring St. Agnes' purity and faith into everyday life. The congregation's efforts in these areas mirrored the broader medieval dedication to merging faith and social duty, as well as St. Agnes' particular commitment to putting her ideals into action.

In addition to the establishment of monastic organizations, St. Agnes' influence during the Middle Ages was visible in the extensive devotional rituals and creative representations that evolved. Pilgrimages to St. Agnes' shrines, such as her basilica in Rome, became popular among medieval Christians who wanted to worship her relics and seek her intercession. The pilgrimage routes, which were embellished with monuments and signs remembering her life and martyrdom, facilitated a deep bond between the devout and the saint. These pilgrimages were not just acts of personal devotion but also manifestations of collective faith, reflecting the widespread veneration for St. Agnes in medieval Christendom.

The Middle Ages art frequently featured episodes from St. Agnes' life, emphasizing her purity and suffering. Churches and cathedrals around Europe were decorated with murals, stained glass windows, and sculptures commemorating her narrative. These creative portrayals acted as both devotional aids and instructional tools, informing the faithful about her virtues and urging them to follow her example. The visual emphasis on St. Agnes' purity and valor maintained her role as a model of Christian virtue while also serving as a potent symbol of faith for the medieval audience.

Furthermore, the medieval liturgical calendar includes feast days and celebrations commemorating St. Agnes, which were commemorated by special services, processions, and prayers. The commemoration of her feast day on January 21st became an opportunity for collective worship and meditation, drawing attention to her life and legacy. These liturgical rituals not only commemorated St. Agnes but also reinforced the principles she represented in the larger context of medieval Christian worship and communal life.

During the Middle Ages, St. Agnes' influence expanded beyond ecclesiastical and artistic domains to encompass the larger cultural environment. Her narrative became a strong symbol of perseverance and faith, resonating with medieval Christians who faced similar hardships and uncertainty. She represented an ideal of purity and perseverance, which inspired and encouraged believers to persevere in their own spiritual journeys and uphold the values she displayed.

In sum, the Middle Ages saw the emergence of monastic orders dedicated to St. Agnes' memory, extensive devotional rituals, and a rich heritage of creative expression. Her impact extended to many facets of medieval life, including monastic communities and pilgrimage rituals, as well as artistic and liturgical expression. These achievements helped to maintain and honor St. Agnes' legacy, ensuring that her example of purity and faith continued to inspire and guide Christians throughout the medieval period and beyond.

Artists and Poets: Depictions of a Saint

St. Agnes' representation in art, poetry, and literature from the medieval period and beyond demonstrates the profound influence her life and virtues had on Christian culture. Her image became a powerful symbol of purity and faith, prompting other artists and writers to interpret her narrative in ways that reflected her long-lasting influence and the ideals she embodied.

In medieval art, St. Agnes was commonly represented with imagery emphasizing her purity and martyrdom. Artists frequently depicted her as a young, tranquil figure, ornamented with symbols such as a lamb, which represented her innocence and purity. This iconography was inspired by the legend of St. Agnes as the "Lamb of God" because of her purity and function as a selfless testament to her faith. These images not only emphasized her virtues, but also inspired viewers by personifying the concepts of devotion and fortitude.

One of St. Agnes's most prominent artistic depictions is her holding a lamb. This sign, derived from her name's Latin meaning "lamb," became a common motif in medieval and Renaissance artworks. In these depictions, St. Agnes is frequently represented cradling a lamb or surrounded by lambs, emphasizing her purity and innocence. Such depictions were intended to highlight her saintly traits and to remind viewers of the purity that should be present in their own lives.

The depiction of her martyrdom is another important part of St. Agnes' representation in art. Artists depicted the dramatic scenes from her trial and death, emphasizing her bravery and strong faith. For example, scenes of her being led to her execution or miraculous happenings surrounding her martyrdom, such as her survival from a fire, were frequently depicted. These visuals emphasized her bravery and the heavenly protection she received, giving viewers a compelling lesson of how to overcome adversity with faith.

In addition to visual art, St. Agnes was an important figure in medieval poetry and literature. Poets and authors were inspired by her story to explore themes of purity, sacrifice, and divine favor. Her life was regularly cited as an example of moral living and spiritual devotion. St. Agnes was honored by medieval songs and hymns that praised her steadfastness and role as an example of Christian virtue.

One famous example is the liturgical hymn "Agnus Dei," which means "Lamb of God" and has been utilized in numerous kinds of Christian devotion. This hymn frequently made reference to St. Agnes, emphasizing her purity and function as a symbol of sacrificial love. Such songs were adopted to cement St. Agnes' tale in the spiritual and liturgical lives of medieval Christians, strengthening her image as a model of virtue.

St. Agnes was also commonly used as a key character in allegories and moral fables. Her life was frequently exploited in these books to communicate moral lessons and spiritual goals through storytelling. Writers used her narrative to show how faith triumphed over worldly temptations and how everlasting life was the ultimate reward. These literary renderings helped to preserve her legacy and inspired people to emulate her values.

Throughout the Renaissance, depictions of St. Agnes evolved to reflect shifting artistic techniques and cultural situations. Renaissance artists, including Raphael and Caravaggio, painted more subtle and dramatic representations of her life, emphasizing the emotional and spiritual components of her story. These works frequently used innovative creative methods, such as chiaroscuro (the use of stark contrasts between light and dark), to heighten the dramatic effect and highlight the divine presence in her life.

In addition to specific artworks, St. Agnes' image has been featured in a variety of public and religious settings. Churches, cathedrals, and chapels devoted to her were decorated with statues, stained glass windows, and murals depicting scenes from her life. These creative portrayals served not only as objects of worship but also as instructional instruments, instructing the faithful on her virtues and urging them to emulate her.

Overall, the portrayal of St. Agnes in art, poetry, and literature illustrates her life and virtues' tremendous influence on Christian culture. Her picture was utilized to transmit powerful themes of purity, faith, and heavenly protection, encouraging countless people to strive for the principles she represented. St. Agnes' legacy has been preserved and cherished via these artistic and literary depictions, which continue to inspire and guide future generations of Christians.

Patroness of the Pure

St. Agnes' role as patroness of the pure, particularly young girls and those seeking chastity, demonstrates her long-lasting impact and deep devotion within Christian tradition. Her life and martyrdom, which were defined by her persistent commitment to purity and faith, have earned her the reputation of a powerful intercessor and an example for those seeking to live by comparable virtues.

From the early Christian era to the present day, St. Agnes has been revered as a special guardian of young girls. Her background, which includes her strong refusal to surrender her religion and her vow to virginity in the face of severe hardship and persecution, makes her an excellent patron for people who strive for purity. In many cultures and traditions, she is revered as a protector of innocence and a guide for young women negotiating life's complications.

St. Agnes' patronage has a tremendous impact on the lives of young girls preparing for maturity. In many Christian communities, St. Agnes is seen as a model of purity and virtue, and her example is utilized to motivate and guide young women in their personal and spiritual development. Her feast day, January 21st, is frequently commemorated with special services and events centered around the themes of purity and chastity, emphasizing her role as a spiritual guide and protector.

In Catholic education and formation, St. Agnes is commonly mentioned as an example of how to lead a virtue-filled life. Her narrative is given to young girls and women as a compelling example of the bravery and courage required to hold onto one's principles in the face of adversity. St. Agnes' life is frequently included in the curricula of schools and religious organizations that educate young women, serving as a source of inspiration and advice for students.

St. Agnes' patronage extends beyond adolescence to people desiring a chaste life. Individuals seeking her intercession strive to uphold their vows of chastity, whether in monastic life or in personal obligations. Religious orders and communities committed to the values of purity and chastity frequently ask her intercession for help and direction on their spiritual journeys.

St. Agnes' worship as patroness of chastity is expressed in a variety of devotional activities and customs. Many people and communities have specific prayers and devotions to request her intercession, asking for her assistance in remaining pure and conquering temptations. These devotions frequently include novenas, specific petitions, and acts of dedication to St. Agnes, which highlight her position as a spiritual champion and protector.

In addition to personal devotion, St. Agnes is celebrated by different organizations and projects that promote chastity and purity. Religious and charity organizations dedicated to empowering young women and pushing for purity values frequently draw inspiration from St. Agnes' example. Her life represents the principles they strive to promote, and her intercession is frequently sought in their efforts to cultivate a culture of respect and honesty.

St. Agnes' impact as patroness of the pure can also be seen in the symbolic use of her image in numerous contexts relating to purity and chastity. Her iconography, which frequently features the lamb and other images of innocence, appears in artwork, jewelry, and religious goods intended to encourage and remind people of her example. These emblems serve as concrete reminders of her virtues and her role as a defender for those who strive to live a pure life.

St. Agnes' legacy as patroness of young girls and those seeking chastity lives on in today's Christian life. Her narrative remains a powerful monument to the virtues of purity and faith, providing inspiration and support to those who struggle to live by these principles. St. Agnes' impact lives on as a source of instruction and encouragement for those wanting to uphold the virtues she displayed, thanks to her ongoing devotion and many forms of honor.

To summarize, St. Agnes' role as patroness of the pure includes her impact on young girls, those desiring chastity, and those committed to leading a virtuous life. Her life and martyrdom have established her as a potent symbol of purity and faith, and her ongoing adoration reflects the high regard in which she is held. St. Agnes' legacy as a guardian of innocence and guide for people striving to keep chastity is still alive and well in Christian tradition, as evidenced by devotional rituals, religious education, and symbolic representations.

Agnes in Our Times

Today, St. Agnes is a source of inspiration and devotion for Catholics all around the world. Despite the centuries since her martyrdom, her message of purity, faith, and courage is still deeply relevant and meaningful today. The methods by which St. Agnes is remembered today demonstrate both her long-lasting legacy and the continued relevance of her virtues in the lives of believers.

Modern devotions to St. Agnes frequently express diverse kinds of prayer, celebration, and community involvement. One of the most visible features of modern devotion is the commemoration of her feast day, January 21st. On this day, churches and communities all across the world commemorate her life with special Masses, processions, and meditations. These liturgical observances emphasize her virtues and provide an opportunity for the faithful to seek her intercession and be inspired by her example.

In addition to liturgical festivities, modern Catholics frequently engage with St. Agnes through individual and communal devotions. Many people incorporate prayers to St. Agnes into their daily spiritual practices, seeking her intercession in concerns of purity, courage, and faith. These prayers are commonly used in personal devotions, novenas, and prayer groups when believers seek her advice and support on their own spiritual journeys.

St. Agnes' influence is also seen in the expanding number of religious communities and organizations dedicated to her memory. These organizations frequently promote the ideals she exemplified, including virginity, fidelity, and dedication to service. For example, some Catholic schools and youth organizations named after her highlight her virtues in their educational and formation activities. These institutions hope that by teaching young people about St. Agnes' life and legacy, they may be inspired to live out the same ideals themselves.

The way St. Agnes' narrative is told in current media reflects her enduring relevance. Several books, essays, and internet tools examine her life and virtues, making her tale more accessible to a new generation of Christians. These resources frequently feature insights on how her example might be applied to current issues, which helps to connect her message with the everyday lives of modern Catholics.

Social media and digital platforms have also played an important role in spreading devotion to St. Agnes. Catholics offer ideas, prayers, and testimonials about her life on blogs, social media platforms, and internet forums. These platforms foster a global conversation about her impact and allow people to interact with one another via their mutual veneration of the saint. Modern media allows her to share her message and communicate with a diverse audience, broadening her reach beyond traditional boundaries.

In addition to personal and communal devotions, St. Agnes' message continues to inspire a variety of humanitarian and social activities. Organizations working on problems such as purity education, youth empowerment, and faith-based outreach frequently utilize her example to influence their efforts. Her life is a tremendous symbol of integrity and resilience, inspiring various initiatives to uphold the principles she embodied and have a beneficial impact on the world.

St. Agnes' portrayal in contemporary art and literature illustrates her enduring importance. Modern artists and writers frequently use her story to explore ideas of purity, courage, and divine protection. These contemporary works offer new views on her life and assist to keep her message relevant and important to today's audiences.

ST. AGNES AND THE LAMB: Symbols Of Purity

The Symbol of the Lamb

The lamb represents a significant aspect of St. Agnes' life and legacy. This iconic image, which is firmly steeped in Christian symbolism, captures crucial characteristics of her purity, sacrifice, and role as a model of virtue.

The lamb is a significant Christian symbol, representing innocence, purity, and sacrifice. This emblem is especially meaningful for St. Agnes because it is associated with her name, which is derived from the Latin word agnus, meaning "lamb." This connection highlights her purity and the sacrificial aspect of her martyrdom.

One of the most well-known depictions of St. Agnes with a lamb is in the visual arts. To represent Mary's innocence and purity, artists frequently picture her carrying a lamb or surrounded by lambs. This imagery refers directly to her name and emphasizes her role as a "Lamb of God," repeating the symbolism of Christ as the ultimate sacrificial lamb. In these depictions, the use of the lamb emphasizes her role as a pure and innocent young woman who, despite her youth, braved persecution with unflinching faith.

The lamb also represents the sacrificial nature of St. Agnes' martyrdom. The life and death of St. Agnes represent a profound act of spiritual offering, much as the lamb in the Old Testament represented sacrifice. Her reluctance to abandon her faith and her fortitude in the face of persecution symbolize the ultimate sacrifice, drawing parallels between the sacrificial lamb of the Jewish Passover and the Christian idea of Christ's sacrifice. In this light, the lamb represents her readiness to devote her life for her values, establishing her as an example of sacrificial love and dedication.

In Christian liturgy and iconography, the lamb is typically connected with redemption and purity. For example, the liturgical expression "Agnus Dei" or "Lamb of God" refers to Christ's sacrifice for humanity's sins. As a result of her martyrdom, St. Agnes is frequently regarded as a symbol of this holy sacrifice. Her association with the lamb highlights the theme of purity and salvation in her story.

The lamb symbol has a deeper theological meaning in Christianity. In the book of Revelation, Christ is depicted as the Lamb who is worthy to open the scroll and bring about humanity's ultimate redemption. The imagery of the lamb as a symbol of Christ's sacrifice and victory over sin and death is reminiscent of St. Agnes' purity and courage. Her life and martyrdom are considered as exemplifying the Christian faith's basic ideals of redemption and spiritual purity.

The lamb's prominent role in St. Agnes' iconography has practical ramifications for devotional practices. For many Christians, the image of St. Agnes with a lamb serves as a visual reminder of the qualities she embodied. She is frequently featured in stained glass windows, sculptures, and religious artwork in churches devoted to her, with the lamb serving as a continual emblem of her purity and sacrifice.

Today, the lamb remains a prominent emblem in devotional materials dedicated to St. Agnes. Religious objects such as medals, prayer cards, and devotional publications frequently depict the lamb in their design, strengthening her connection to purity and sacrifice. These symbols continue to inspire and remind believers of her qualities and the spiritual lessons she embodies.

Overall, the lamb symbolizes St. Agnes' innocence, purity, and selfless love. It serves as a powerful reminder of her unwavering conviction and the ultimate cost she paid for her beliefs. The lamb is a major symbol in commemorating St. Agnes' legacy through art, liturgy, and personal devotion, representing her role as a paragon of virtue and a testimony to the timeless principles of purity and sacrifice.

Feast Day Traditions

St. Agnes' feast day, January 21st, is observed with a variety of traditional rites and customs that reflect her importance in Christian devotion as well as the long-standing respect of her life and virtues. One of the most significant customs associated with her feast is the blessing of the lambs, which serves a unique role in the church's liturgical life and emphasizes the symbolic link between St. Agnes and the lamb.

The tradition of blessing the lambs stems from both St. Agnes' symbolism and the Church's practical requirements. On her feast day, the Pope blesses lambs at the Basilica of St. Agnes in Rome. This practice stretches back to the early centuries of Christianity and has evolved into a meaningful ceremony emphasizing St. Agnes' symbolism as an example of purity and sacrifice.

The ceremony includes the blessing of lambs, whose wool is then used to make palliums, a particular vestment worn by Popes and Archbishops. The pallium, composed of wool from these blessed lambs, represents the church's pastoral care and power. By blessing the lambs and utilizing their wool for this sacred purpose, the Church connects St. Agnes' characteristics of purity, innocence, and sacrifice to the Church's ongoing mission and leadership.

The ceremony is very symbolic, serving to strengthen the spiritual bond between St. Agnes and the larger ecclesiastical heritage. The lamb, a symbol of innocence and sacrifice, represents St. Agnes' purity and readiness to devote her life to her religion. The Church commemorates St. Agnes by introducing the lamb into liturgical practice, while also drawing on her example to promote pastoral care and leadership in the Church.

The blessing of the lambs is performed with considerable attention and ceremonial detail. During the feast day celebration, the Pope or another high-ranking religious figure blesses in a solemn and formal manner. The lambs are transported to the basilica, frequently accompanied by prayers and hymns emphasizing the importance of the event. The blessed lambs are then cared for until their wool is collected and processed to make the palliums.

This custom also brings the devout closer together with their faith's symbolic elements. The link between the blessed lambs and the palliums worn by the Pope and archbishops acts as a physical reminder of the Church's continuity and the continued importance of St. Agnes' virtues. It bridges the past and present, linking St. Agnes' martyrdom to the Church's current leadership and mission.

In addition to the lamb blessing, St. Agnes' feast day is commemorated with various traditional events and rituals. These may include special Masses, processions, and public devotions to St. Agnes. The faithful gather to honor her life, reflect on her virtues, and pray for her intercession. These festivities frequently include Scripture readings, songs, and homilies centered on the themes of purity, sacrifice, and unwavering faith.

St. Agnes' feast day also allows for reflection on her legacy and the impact her life had on the Christian community. The ceremonies and celebrations reaffirm the church's dedication to the values she represented and encourage the faithful to follow in her footsteps.

In modern times, the customs surrounding St. Agnes' feast day continue to inspire and interest the faithful. The blessing of the lambs is still a popular tradition that connects St. Agnes' symbolism to the practical and spiritual aspects of church life. It serves as a reminder of her virtues' timeless relevance and the Church's ongoing responsibility to defend the principles she represented.

Finally, the feast day customs honoring St. Agnes, particularly the blessing of the lambs, reflect the profound symbolism and significance of her life and virtues. These rites celebrate her memory, connect her example to the

Church's leadership, and allow the faithful to participate in the spiritual and symbolic aspects of her legacy. The Church continues to commemorate and be inspired by St. Agnes through these activities, reaffirming her long-lasting influence on the Christian tradition.

Agnes as a Model of Sacrificial Love

St. Agnes is a powerful example of sacrificial love, one that goes beyond personal comfort and earthly ties to embrace the divine will with unshakable confidence. Her life and death exemplify the essence of sacrificial love, making her an excellent role model for Christians wanting to comprehend and practice this profound virtue.

St. Agnes demonstrated a remarkable commitment to Christ from an early age, based on her deep love and devotion. Her resolve to stay chaste and devote her life entirely to God was more than just a personal choice; it was a profound act of sacrificial love. In an era where social position and marriage were valued highly, Agnes' vow of chastity was a daring and courageous expression of her love for Christ above all other concerns.

The sacrificial quality of Agnes' devotion is starkly demonstrated by her readiness to face persecution and death rather than abandon her beliefs. Her strong determination to uphold her Christian convictions in the face of great pressure and impending death demonstrates the depth of her love. Her bravery in the face of such adversity demonstrates a genuine and pure dedication to Christ, revealing that her love was more than a feeling; it was a lived reality that permeated every part of her life.

Agnes' dedication to selfless love is also obvious in how she handled her martyrdom. Her death was not a passive resignation but an intentional and purposeful decision to follow Christ till the end. The hardships and tortures she underwent demonstrated her unwavering love and faith in the promise of eternal life. Her determination to suffer and die rather than compromise her beliefs exemplifies the transformative power of sacrificial love, demonstrating that true love frequently entails personal sacrifice and the willingness to endure pain for the greater good.

The concept of sacrificial love is profoundly rooted in Christian theology, and it is frequently associated with Christ's ultimate act of love, his sacrifice on the cross. St. Agnes' life mirrors this holy example, reflecting the same self-giving love that Christ exemplified. Agnes displays Christian love by choosing to give her life rather than compromise her religion.

Agnes' tale also has important implications for contemporary Christians who want to live out their faith. Her example encourages believers to reflect on their own lives and how they can exemplify sacrificial love in their own circumstances. Whether through acts of service, personal sacrifices, or standing fast in their convictions in the face of adversity' life inspires modern Christians to consider the depth of their commitment and to seek methods to live out their religion with the same courage and devotion she demonstrated.

When meditating on Agnes' sacrificial love, it is crucial to remember that it is not limited to spectacular gestures or dramatic acts of valor. It can also be found in the daily decisions and sacrifices that Christians make. Agnes' life demonstrates that sacrificial love frequently consists of a series of little, thoughtful deeds that reveal a devotion to Christ and others. Her example inspires Christians to approach their relationships, obligations, and obstacles with compassion and selflessness, striving to reflect Christ's love in every part of their lives.

St. Agnes' narrative continues to inspire and challenge believers, demonstrating the ongoing impact of her sacrificial devotion. Her story is a striking reminder of the importance of selfless love and the willingness to make sacrifices for a greater good. Christians are encouraged by her example to embrace the transformative power of sacrificial love and to seek ways to manifest it in their own lives.

Finally, St. Agnes exemplifies sacrificial love through her persistent dedication to Christ and willingness to face pain and death for the sake of her faith. Her life provides a compelling example for Christians wanting to comprehend and embody this profound virtue. By reflecting on her example, believers are encouraged to embody the essence of sacrificial love in their own lives, finding inspiration from her courage and commitment as they strive to follow Christ with the same level of devotion.

Living Purity in a Corrupt World

Living a life of purity and love in a morally corrupt world can be a difficult challenge, but it is one that many people choose to embrace. St. Agnes' example serves as both inspiration and practical guidance for modern readers seeking to keep their ideals and faith in the face of contemporary society's complexities and challenges.

Here are some practical methods to nurture purity and love in today's world:

1. **Develop a Strong Spiritual Foundation**

A strong and continuous spiritual life is required to retain purity and love in a corrupt environment. Practice regular prayer, meditation, and thought to deepen your relationship with God. Regular attendance at the sacraments, such as Eucharist and Confession, can also bring spiritual nourishment and guidance. Grounding yourself in your faith helps you establish resilience in the face of potential hardships and temptations.

2. **Set clear moral boundaries.**

Establish and sustain clear moral boundaries that are consistent with your values and beliefs. This is making intentional decisions about what you consume, both physically and psychologically. Be aware of your entertainment, conversations, and surroundings. Setting boundaries creates a place that supports your dedication to purity while also allowing you to avoid situations that could lead you astray.

3. Embrace a life of service and compassion.

Living out purity and love frequently entails showing kindness and compassion to others. Look for ways to help others in need, whether through volunteer work, charitable contributions, or simple acts of kindness in your daily contacts. Service not only benefits others, but it also reinforces your own beliefs and keeps you focused on the good things in life rather than being consumed by negativity or corruption.

4. Create a supportive community.

Surround yourself with people who share your ideals and encourage your dedication to purity and love. This may be friends, family, or members of your faith community. Engaging with individuals that encourage and uplift you can create a powerful support system while also keeping you accountable on your journey. Share your problems and triumphs with trusted people who can provide advice and encouragement.

5. Practice self-reflection and accountability.

Regular self-reflection allows you to analyze how well you are living your values and where you may need to make changes. Set aside time for personal reflection, and be truthful with yourself about your behaviors and beliefs. Accountability partners, such as friends, mentors, or spiritual advisors, can help you keep on track and offer assistance in areas where you may struggle.

6. Concentrate on personal growth and development.

Strive for personal improvement in all facets of your life. Pursue study, self-improvement, and spiritual development to better your knowledge and abilities. Growth in these areas can help you navigate problems more efficiently while still maintaining a feeling of purpose and direction. By constantly striving to be the finest version of yourself, you strengthen your commitment to live a pure, loving life.

7. **Seek forgiveness and renewal.**

Recognize that living a life of purity and love is a journey, and it is normal to experience setbacks along the way. When you fall short, seek forgiveness and turn these experiences into chances for growth and regeneration. Accept the grace and mercy afforded through confession and reconciliation, and see each day as an opportunity to start over.

8. **Advocate of Justice and Integrity**

Advocate for fairness and integrity in your interactions and in the larger community. This could include speaking up against injustice, promoting ethical practices, or providing a voice for those who are disenfranchised. By pushing for what is right, you help to create a more just and compassionate world that reflects the purity and love that St. Agnes represented.

9. **Live with intention and purpose**

Approach each day with intention and purpose, and set goals that are consistent with your values and beliefs. Make mindful decisions that reflect your dedication to purity and love and avoid developing habits or routines that may jeopardize your values. Living intentionally allows you to live a meaningful and faith-based life.

10. **Draw inspiration from saints and spiritual figures.**

Look to the lives of saints and spiritual leaders for inspiration and advice. Their stories of faith, purity, and love provide essential lessons and can be great motivators in your own journey. Reflect on their experiences and apply their wisdom to your own life, aiming to replicate their values and incorporate their teachings into your everyday routine.

Living a life of purity and love in a morally corrupt world necessitates intentionality, self-discipline, and a solid spiritual foundation. You may navigate modern life while remaining faithful to your beliefs by building a deep relationship with God, setting clear moral boundaries, performing acts of service, and finding support from a like-minded group. Drawing inspiration from St. Agnes and other spiritual figures can help you stay motivated and inspired as you attempt to live a pure and loving life.

LESSONS FROM ST. AGNES FOR TODAY'S CHRISTIAN

Purity of Heart in a Secular Society

Maintaining purity of heart and strong faith in an increasingly secular culture might be difficult, but it remains an essential component of living a Christian life. St. Agnes' example offers timeless advice for negotiating today's society, where secular standards frequently conflict with Catholic beliefs.

Here are several strategies to maintain purity of heart and religion in a secular society:

1. Ground yourself in spiritual practices.

In today's secular environment, where distractions and competing ideals abound, it is critical to establish regular spiritual activities. Daily prayer, meditation, and Bible study are essential for sustaining purity of heart. These practices assist in strengthening your faith and provide an opportunity to reflect on your ideals in the face of external influences. By setting aside time each day to cultivate your spiritual life, you lay a solid foundation that supports your beliefs and leads your actions.

2. Cultivate inner virtue.

Purity of heart starts with building inner virtue. This includes cultivating values like humility, integrity, and compassion. Consider your attitudes and behaviors, and work to line them with Christian principles. Engage in self-examination to find areas where you may improve, and concentrate on embodying values that reflect a pure and compassionate heart. Focusing on inner virtue allows you to navigate secular influences while remaining clear and committed to your convictions.

3. Select Your Influences Wisely

In a secular culture, media, social networks, and other forces may frequently promote ideals that contradict Christian teachings. Be mindful of the stuff you consume and the people you associate with. Surround yourself with people who are encouraging and supportive of your faith. This could include selecting media that is consistent with your values, participating in communities that share your ideas, and avoiding circumstances that weaken your spiritual commitment.

4. Practice discipline.

Discernment is vital for keeping the heart pure. This entails making deliberate, prayerful judgments about how you interact with the world. When faced with decisions or dilemmas, consult Scripture, prayer, and spiritual counselors. Practicing discernment allows you to negotiate challenging situations with clarity and keep your heart connected with your beliefs. Discernment enables you to act with integrity and adhere to your ideals even when confronted with secular influences.

5. Engage in Meaningful Community.

Belonging to a faith group offers invaluable support and encouragement. Participate actively in your church or religious groups, including worship, study, and fellowship. Being part of a group that shares your values provides support and accountability. It also offers opportunities for mutual support and growth, which can help you stay dedicated to your faith and preserve a pure heart in a secular environment.

6. Reflect Christian Values in Daily Life.

Living out your faith in everyday deeds deepens your dedication to purity of spirit. Reflect Christian principles in the way you interact with others, make decisions, and deal with obstacles. In your personal and professional connections, demonstrate kindness, honesty, and humility. Integrating your faith into your daily life demonstrates that purity of heart is more than an internal trait; it is a lived embodiment of your beliefs.

7. Stand firm in your convictions.

Maintaining purity of heart takes courage and conviction, especially in a secular environment where Christian principles may be questioned. Be willing to remain solid in your views, even if it is challenging. This could include having unpleasant conversations, making countercultural decisions, or facing criticism. Standing firm demonstrates the power of your faith and the courage that St. Agnes exemplified in her life.

8. Seek continuous spiritual growth.

Continue to grow spiritually via study, thought, and involvement with your faith. Attend religious education programs, study spiritual books, and seek advice from mentors or spiritual leaders. Growing in your understanding and practice of faith strengthens your commitment and improves your ability to live with a pure heart. Spiritual growth enables you to manage secular forces with knowledge and commitment.

9. Embrace God's grace.

Recognize that sustaining purity of heart is a journey in which God's grace plays an important part. When you face difficulties or moments of weakness, look to God for support and forgiveness. Accepting God's grace enables you to move on with renewed determination and humility. Trust in God's strength and the transformative power of grace as you strive to live a life that reflects His love and purity.

10. Share your faith with others.

Living with purity of heart entails sharing your beliefs with others. Use your actions and words to demonstrate the transformative power of faith. Engage in discussions about your beliefs and offer support and encouragement to others who are striving to live out their faith. Sharing your faith helps to promote a better knowledge and respect of Christian principles in a secular environment.

Finally, preserving a pure heart in a secular world necessitates deliberate effort based on spiritual disciplines, inner virtue, and discernment. You can overcome secular obstacles while being committed to your faith by carefully selecting your influences, participating in meaningful communities, and expressing Christian principles in your daily lives. St. Agnes' example is a powerful guide, reminding us of the strength and grace available to those who strive to live with a pure and compassionate heart among the difficulties of today's world.

Courage in the Face of Persecution

Courage in the face of persecution is a defining feature of the Christian faith, demonstrating a strong commitment to God's truth and ideals in the face of external pressures and threats. St. Agnes' persistent bravery in the face of terrible persecution teaches modern Christians valuable lessons about dealing with hostility to their faith.

<u>Here's a thought on the fortitude required to be firm in religion, even in difficult circumstances</u>:

1. Embracing the Call of Courage

Courage is frequently portrayed as a heroic quality, but for Christians, it is a necessary response to the call to fidelity. St. Agnes demonstrated exceptional bravery by refusing to surrender her faith in the face of harsh persecution, and modern believers are encouraged to embrace courage in their own settings. This entails remaining solid in one's beliefs even in the face of criticism, animosity, or personal loss. In the Christian perspective, courage is defined as acting with resolve and trust in the face of dread.

2. Drawing Strength from Faith.

The ability to face persecution stems from a profound and abiding faith in God. For Christians, faith is the foundation that offers the fortitude to face adversity. St. Agnes' strength stemmed from her deep faith in Christ and the hope of eternal life. Similarly, modern Christians can find courage in facing obstacles by drawing on their religion, prayer, meditation, and the support of their faith community. Individuals facing adversity can be sustained and strengthened by their faith in God's presence and promises.

3. The Role of Spiritual Preparation

When facing persecution with courage, preparation is essential. Spiritual preparation entails developing a strong faith via regular engagement with Scripture, prayer, and spiritual activities. By immersing oneself in Christ's teachings and the examples of saints such as Agnes, believers lay a foundation of strength and understanding that may be drawn on in times of adversity. Spiritual preparedness includes being intellectually and emotionally prepared to confront hardships, as well as realizing that persecution can take many forms, ranging from subtle prejudice to overt antagonism.

4. Learning from the Martyrs

Martyrs' lives, including St. Agnes', serve as outstanding examples of how to face adversity with courage. Their stories are not simply historical descriptions but living testimony that inspires and educates. Reflecting on the experiences of martyrs helps believers understand the nature of persecution and how faith can provide strength. Studying these experiences can help modern Christians understand how to handle their own problems and find strength in their convictions.

5. Cultivating a Spirit of Resolution

Courage in the face of persecution necessitates a spirit of resolve—a firm dedication to one's ideas no matter the cost. This resolution is not easy to obtain; it is built via consistent practice and reinforcement of one's values. In everyday life, this involves choosing decisions that reflect your religion, standing up for what is right, and refusing to compromise your convictions even when it is inconvenient or difficult. Christians who cultivate a spirit of resolution can confront persecution with a strong sense of purpose and determination.

6. Relying on Community Support

During times of persecution, faith-based support can be a source of immense strength and encouragement. Just as St. Agnes' fortitude was bolstered by her faith and the testimony of others, modern believers can benefit from the solidarity and encouragement of their faith communities. Engaging with people who share your values provides emotional support, practical assistance, and a sense of belonging. Community support allows people to feel less alienated and more empowered to face issues collectively.

7. Finding Courage through Witness

Standing firm in religion is a great testimony for others. When Christians face persecution with courage, they not only stand firm in their convictions, but they also provide witness to the strength and reality of their religion. This witness has the potential to inspire and encourage others, resulting in a ripple effect that goes beyond the immediate context of persecution. By boldly living out their faith, believers contribute to a greater narrative of hope and resilience that has the power to impact and lift others.

8. Embracing the Call of Love

Courage involves love and compassion in the face of opposition, not just confrontation. St. Agnes' courage stemmed from her love for Christ and commitment to following His teachings. In current situations, this is responding to persecution with love and forgiveness rather than wrath or resentment. By embracing the call to love, Christians can demonstrate a different approach to adversity that represents the gospel's essential message.

9. Understanding the purpose of trials

Persecution and hardships, however terrible, can serve a larger purpose in the Christian life. They promote growth, strengthen faith, and improve character. Understanding that adversities are part of a broader divine design can provide believers with a feeling of purpose and optimism. By viewing obstacles through this lens, Christians can find significance in their experiences and gain strength from the knowledge that their suffering is not in vain.

10. Trusting God's sovereignty

Finally, courage in the face of adversity is based on trust in God's sovereignty. Believing that God is in control and that everything works out for the best can bring a tremendous amount of calm and confidence. St. Agnes' courage stemmed from her belief that God's plan was greater than any earthly struggle. Modern believers who trust in God's sovereignty can confront persecution with the knowledge that they are in divine hands and that their faithfulness will be rewarded.

The Role of Women in the Church

St. Agnes' life and legacy serve as a powerful inspiration for modern Catholic women, demonstrating how a commitment to faith and purity may shape and enhance their positions in the Church and the world. Her example serves as a beacon for embracing and improving women's contributions in all aspects of life, underscoring their critical position in the church's mission and society.

Here's a look at how St. Agnes' example might inspire contemporary Catholic women:

1. Embracing personal calls

St. Agnes' unshakeable devotion and commitment to her faith demonstrate the importance of accepting one's own calling. Her life demonstrates a deep knowledge of her spiritual destiny, even in the face of severe adversity. Modern Catholic women can learn from Agnes' example to discern and embrace their own callings, whether within the Church, in their careers, or in their communities. Women can make an important contribution to the church's mission and societal development by acknowledging and appreciating their particular responsibilities and gifts.

2. Lead with faith and courage

Agnes' courage in the face of persecution exemplifies the strength that comes from a strong faith and conviction. Catholic women today are called to lead with comparable faith and courage, whether as church leaders, professionals, or in their personal lives. Drawing on Agnes' example, women can fearlessly take up leadership roles, speak for justice, and defend Christian ideals in difficult situations. Her life exemplifies how faith-based leadership can inspire others and bring about significant change.

3. Contributing to the Church's mission

St. Agnes' unshakable faith, even at the expense of her life, demonstrates the necessity of contributing to the church's mission. Catholic women contribute significantly to the Church's efforts in evangelization, education, and social justice. Women's involvement in numerous ministries, ranging from teaching religious education to conducting social outreach initiatives, demonstrates the many ways in which they contribute to the Church's mission. Agnes' example inspires women to actively participate in these roles, using their abilities and passions to advance the church's mission around the world.

4. Living a Life with Integrity and Purity

Agnes' dedication to purity and integrity offers an example of how Catholic women can live out their religion authentically and gracefully. In a world fraught with moral ambiguity, her example is a striking testament to leading a life of integrity and purity. Catholic women might be inspired by Agnes' adherence to her ideals and use her example to shape their own decisions and interactions. Living with integrity not only improves one's personal religious journey but it also serves as an effective witness to others.

5. Fostering Community and Support

Agnes' religion and community reinforced her fortitude, and this serves as a lesson for current Catholic women. Creating supporting groups inside the church and beyond is critical for personal and community growth. Women may cultivate cultures of encouragement and mutual support, allowing religion and fellowship to develop. Women may increase their collective impact, support one another in their roles, and contribute to a more dynamic and united church community by banding together.

6. Championing the Dignity of Women

St. Agnes' life promotes women's inherent dignity and critical role in the church and society. Her example can encourage modern Catholic women to advocate for women's dignity and rights in a variety of settings. This includes advocating for gender equality, empowering women's leadership, and addressing issues of injustice and inequality. By defending women's dignity, Catholic women uphold the Christian faith's core values of respect and fairness.

7. Participating in charitable and service acts

Agnes' life exemplifies a deep devotion to charity and service, both of which are fundamental components of Christian living. Modern Catholic women might follow her example by performing acts of kindness and service in their communities. This involves volunteering, helping those in need, and campaigning for social justice. Women who actively participate in service-oriented activities contribute to the church's mission and have a visible impact on the world, exemplifying St. Agnes's love and compassion.

8. Fostering Spiritual Growth

Agnes' unwavering faith and commitment to her spiritual life demonstrate the value of continual spiritual development. Prayer, reflection, and participation in the sacraments are critical for Catholic women's spiritual development. St. Agnes' example inspires women to develop their connection with God and seek ongoing spiritual growth. This commitment to spiritual growth enhances their ability to fulfill their responsibilities and make significant contributions to the church and society.

9. Inspiring Future Generations

St. Agnes' story inspires future generations of Catholic women. Her life narrative can be an effective instrument for teaching young women the importance of faith, courage, and devotion. Catholic women can inspire and mentor future generations by sharing their experiences and stories, assisting them in understanding and accepting their own positions in the Church and the world. This generational transfer of faith and values guarantees that St. Agnes' example remains relevant and inspiring.

10. Balancing Faith with Professional Life

Many modern Catholic women balance work and faith. St. Agnes' life teaches how it is possible to maintain one's convictions while partaking in diverse facets of life. Women can be inspired by her example to balance their career and spiritual obligations. This balance allows people to honestly live out their faith while also making valuable contributions in their respective professions.

St. Agnes' example serves as a powerful inspiration for modern Catholic women, encouraging them to embrace their roles with faith, courage, and dedication. Catholic women can carry on St. Agnes' legacy by leading with integrity, contributing to the Church's mission, cultivating supportive communities, and advocating for women's dignity. Her life is a tremendous monument to the impact that dedicated, faith-filled women can have on the Church and the world, inspiring others to follow her lead and live out their own callings with grace and purpose.

Embracing the Cross with Joy

Embracing the cross with joy is a profound component of Christian faith, and St. Agnes' life exemplifies how to face hardship and suffering with unbroken joy and faith. Her journey, marked by significant trials and ultimate sacrifice, encourages current Christians to take a similar approach to their own struggles. Here's a perspective on how to face personal challenges with the same joy and faith as St. Agnes' journey:

1. Understanding the Cross as a Path for Transformation

For St. Agnes, the cross was more than just a symbol of suffering; it was a route to spiritual transformation and ultimate unity with Christ. Accepting one's cross with joy entails acknowledging that trials and tribulations can be chances for growth and faith development. When viewed through this lens, pain becomes a tool for growing closer to God, refining character, and experiencing profound spiritual development. Modern readers can draw inspiration from Agnes' example by recognizing their own hardships as part of a divine plan for personal and spiritual growth.

2. Find Joy in Suffering

St. Agnes' exceptional capacity to endure persecution and death with pleasure demonstrates the depth of her faith and devotion to Christ. Embracing the cross with pleasure entails discovering a deep sense of serenity and purpose, even in the face of suffering. This joy stems not from the pain itself, but from knowing that God is there and working through it. Christians are called to experience this joy by focusing on God's eternal promises and the hope of resurrection. Individuals who cultivate this perspective can face their crosses with a heart full of joy and faith in God's ultimate plan.

3. Accepting Suffering as a Form of Participation in Christ's Passion.

Christians join in Christ's suffering and sacrifice by joyfully accepting their crosses. St. Agnes' willingness to suffer for the sake of her faith parallels Christ's trip to the cross. This engagement allows one to enhance their relationship with Christ and connect their suffering to His redemptive work. Understanding suffering as a way of joining in Christ's passion allows believers to approach their own challenges with purpose and spiritual significance.

4. Developing a Spirit of Gratitude

Developing a spirit of thankfulness is an important part of joyfully accepting the cross. Despite the pain and struggle, St. Agnes' joy sprang from her gratitude for the opportunity to witness to her religion. Modern Christians might take a similar stance, expressing gratitude for how hardship brings them closer to God and develops their faith. Gratitude moves the emphasis away from the burden of the cross and toward the gifts and spiritual insights that result from it. Individuals who cultivate a grateful heart can discover joy even in the midst of adversity.

5. Finding strength in prayer and sacraments

Prayer and the sacraments are essential sources of strength and grace when facing the cross. St. Agnes' unwavering faith was maintained by her deep relationship with God, which was supported by prayer and the spiritual practices of her time. Modern Christians can use these similar sources of strength to face their own hardships with joy. Regular prayer, attendance at the Eucharist, and other sacramental practices provide spiritual nutrition and support, allowing people to face their challenges with fresh hope and confidence.

6. Supporting one another on the journey

The journey of joyfully accepting the cross does not need to be undertaken alone. The greater Christian community backed St. Agnes' courage and faith. In the same spirit, modern Christians are required to encourage, pray for, and provide practical assistance to one another during difficult times. They can find delight in mutual support and solidarity when they band together as a community to share the burdens of their crosses. This social aspect of faith boosts people's resolve and delight when facing challenges.

7. Reflecting on the ultimate victory

St. Agnes' example teaches believers that the cross is not the end but rather a gateway to ultimate victory. Her suffering resulted in a deep spiritual triumph, confirming the promise of eternal life with Christ. Embracing one's cross with joy entails keeping the eventual victory in perspective, acknowledging that current sufferings are fleeting in comparison to the eternal joy that awaits. Christians might find the ability to bear suffering with hope and joy by remembering that their hardships are but a prelude to a larger and ultimate victory.

8. Living the Example of the Saints

The lives of saints, particularly St. Agnes, provide specific examples of how to face pain with joy. Their stories of perseverance and optimism in the face of adversity inspire and guide modern believers. Studying and reflecting on the saints' lives can help Christians face their own trials with joy and resilience. The saints demonstrate how to embrace suffering with grace and faith.

9. Integrating faith into everyday life.

Embracing the cross with joy entails incorporating faith into daily living, viewing all elements of life through the prism of faith. St. Agnes' example demonstrates that even in banal or everyday elements of life, people can find ways to live their religion with joy and commitment. Christians can turn regular obstacles and obligations into opportunities for spiritual growth and witness by engaging them with a glad heart and a strong sense of faith.

10: Celebrating Faith's Journey

Finally, embracing the cross with joy entails celebrating the faith journey and acknowledging how God uses trials to bring about spiritual growth and transformation. St. Agnes' life exemplifies the joy that can be found in walking faithfully with God during every stage of life. Christians are encouraged to celebrate their own journeys, finding delight in the ways God works in their lives, even when they face difficulties. Celebrating this journey emphasizes the idea that joy and faith may coexist with sorrow, resulting in a more profound spiritual life.

Finally, St. Agnes strongly exemplifies the transformational quality of Christian faith: joyfully embracing the cross. Christians can follow Agnes' example of approaching their own crosses with faith and joy by understanding the cross as a path to transformation, finding joy in suffering, participating in Christ's passion, cultivating gratitude, drawing strength from prayer, supporting one another, reflecting on ultimate victory, learning from saints, integrating faith into everyday life, and celebrating the journey. Her life acts as a beacon, indicating that joy and sorrow may coexist and that accepting the cross with a glad heart leads to a more profound and enriching spiritual journey.

Made in the USA
Columbia, SC
01 March 2025